The Lost Children

This book is dedicated to all our Old People who never saw their children again and to all our children who never came home.

The Lost Children

Thirteen Australians taken from their Aboriginal families tell of the struggle to find their natural parents

Edited by
Coral Edwards & Peter Read

DOUBLEDAY
Sydney Auckland New York Toronto London

THE LOST CHILDREN
A DOUBLEDAY BOOK
First published in Australia and New Zealand in 1989 by Doubleday
Reprinted 1992, 1997.

National Library of Australia
Cataloguing-in-Publication Entry

The Lost children
ISBN 0 86824 384 1.

(1). Aborigines, Australian—Children—Biography. (2). Aborigines, Australian—Institutional care—Biography. 3. Foster children—Australia—Biography. (4). Aborigines, Australian—Social conditions. I. Edwards, Coral. II. Read, Peter, 1945–

362.7'979913'0922

Doubleday/Bantam books are published by

Transworld Publishers (Aust) Pty Limited
15–25 Helles Avenue, Moorebank, NSW 2170

Transworld Publishers (NZ) Limited
3 William Pickering Drive, Albany, Auckland

Transworld Publishers (UK) Limited
61–63 Uxbridge Road, Ealing, London W5 5SA

Bantam Doubleday Dell Publishing Group Inc.
666 Fifth Avenue, New York, New York 10103

Cover and text design by Trevor Hood
Typeset by Midland Typesetters, Victoria
Printed by The Book Printer, Victoria

10 9 8 7 6 5 4 3

CONTENTS

To become a person complete;
A woman becoming whole.
Black and Beautiful, for the first
time I listen
To the yearning of my soul.

Pauline McLeod

Foreword

I read the manuscript of *The Lost Children* eagerly, anxious to take in the experiences of other Aboriginal people who had suffered under the same policies as my family. There were, of course, many parallels. Deceit and lies on behalf of government departments; sadness, confusion, lack of identity; breakdown of family ties and culture. The story of my own family is not unique. It is echoed thousands of times over the length and breadth of Australia. It is important for us to discuss and detail such things; to reclaim the past, our families, ourselves; to have something to be; a framework within which we can exist, learn, be proud. In the telling we assert the validity of our own experiences and we call the silence of two hundred years a lie. And it is important for you, the listener, because like it or not, we are a part of you. We have to find a way of living together in this country, and that will only come when our hearts, minds and wills are set towards reconciliation. It will only come when thousands of stories have been spoken and listened to with understanding.

The people in this book are engaged in a process of reconciliation with their past, themselves, their families and the Aboriginal community at large. Reconciliation brings wholeness and peace, but the process itself is painful, angry and frustrating. Reconciliation takes time and patience. For those with the time to read and the patience to listen, I commend this book.

Sally Morgan

Introduction

In Australia today there may be one hundred thousand people of Aboriginal descent who do not know their families or communities. They are the people, or the descendants of people, who were removed from their families by a variety of white people for a variety of reasons. They do not know where they come from; some do not even know they are of Aboriginal descent.

This book is the story of a minute fraction of the black children who were raised by white people, some with love and some without love. As they grew up, they were expected to think white, to act white, and in the end to be white. They are united by the common bond that, as adults, they set out to find their families and, in doing so, began to find a new personality, identity and culture.

The removal of Aboriginal children from their parents has been a policy in all states at different times. In New South Wales the Cootamundra Home for Aboriginal Girls and the Kinchela Home for Aboriginal Boys are the best known of several institutions. The Colebrook Home in South Australia and the 'Half-Caste Institution' in Alice Springs were similar institutions specifically designed to raise and socialise Aboriginal children. The people whose stories are reproduced here grew up mainly in New South Wales within the last sixty years, and are members of the organisation Link-Up. In coming to this organisation, which attempts to unite separated families, they wanted to find both their families and their identity as Koories (as New South Wales Aborigines are known to each other). Most of them have been able to do so.

Probably the origin of the practice of separating black children from their parents lay in the desire to turn them into 'useful' citizens. The earliest Aboriginal institutions in Australia, where parents were at first allowed to live nearby, were set up to teach the Anglican virtues of obedience, punctuality, thriftiness and hard work. We still have a daily timetable for the children at the Blacktown institution in 1827 which, though not excessive for those days of workhouse and poor relief, indicates that what the missionaries wanted was a new generation of willing workers:

Schedule:

1. The children to be up and dressed by 6 and set to work.
2. To wash themselves at ½ past 7 go to Prayers and Breakfast at 8.
3. To work till 10 o'clock.
4. To wash and go to school from 10 till 12 write one Copy read half an hour cypher 1 Hour.
5. To dine at ¼ after 12 and play till 1.
6. To school at 1 read and cypher till 2.
7. To work from 2 till 6 the boys at carpentering the girls sewing and knitting.
8. To play and wash and be ready for supper at 7.
9. To Prayers at ½ past 7 and to be in bed at 8.

This was the more positive side of the missionaries' work. They wanted to create an Aboriginal working class and present it to those whites of the colony who thought Aborigines were little better than animals. 'Useful' work demonstrated, so they thought, that Aborigines were capable of 'civilisation'. Like most institutions of the time, we know more about how the Blacktown institution started than how it finished, but it is likely that since the parents were allowed to see their children from time to time and the instructors were not unkind, a few children learned to sew or build.

But there was also a negative side which hardened when the missionaries were confronted by parents who wished to take their children away from the schools. The missionaries' answer was to separate the children, usually by trickery or force. Parents who allowed their children to go to the dormitory were allowed access to them only irregularly or never. By 1850 all the half-dozen missions which had come and gone in eastern Australia had, at one time or another, tried to raise Aboriginal children separated from their parents. They pursued the policy so hard that in some cases the black populations living at or near the missions simply went away. In 1838 at Wellington, in midwestern New South Wales, there was an ugly scene in which a missionary and two constables chased a woman, screaming and clutching her baby, into another missionary's house, then seized the child and took her off to the infants' dormitory. Next day the whole Aboriginal camp left and the work of the Wellington missionaries was never the same again. We know no more about most of the children of these institutions than their names and whether they physically survived the trauma of separation. Probably what they endured emotionally was not very different from the feelings of loss, anger, bewilderment or grief apparent in this book.

The separation of Aboriginal children from their families, therefore, was not an invention of the twentieth century, although its scale before this was modest. Probably by 1850 no more than 300 children had been separated and raised as white as a matter of formal policy. Whatever the effect on the children and the parents involved, enforced separation in the nineteenth century was not the catastrophe to Aboriginal civilisation that it was in the twentieth. For the first hundred years after the invasion the missionaries maintained that black children could be brought to the same level as white labourers and maids if they were trained properly, and the doubters maintained that it was best to let the Aboriginal population die out of its own accord. But most of the children stayed at home.

The turning point that divides the first hundred years of white settlement from the second, and the mostly humanitarian motivations of child separation from the mostly political, was this very question of Aboriginal population. The whites began to realise that the blacks, after all, were not dying out as they had expected.

It is probable that the part-Aboriginal population—that is, the people of part-white descent who lived with and identified as Aborigines—began to increase after 1850, but because the whites were not well established in the rural regions, they didn't notice. It was not until the 1870s and 1880s that the whites who were vocal enough to complain to the government began to draw attention to the black populations gathering around the newly established towns. It was the same sort of people—the lawyers, bankers, newspaper editors and clerks—who drew the attention of the politicians to the Sydney camps at La Perouse, Manly and Circular Quay. They demanded that the government take measures to control what to the whites had suddenly become an increasing rather than a decreasing problem.

So the century of Aboriginal persecution which began with the establishment of the Aborigines Protection Board in 1883 was in many ways the answer to the complaints and demands of the whites who were confronted with Aborigines near their towns. Not all the Board members were persecutors; like those who established the early Sydney schools, their intentions were at first fairly benevolent. But by 1900 the parameters were set. The Board reasoned that if the Aboriginal population, characterised in some quarters as a 'wild race of half-castes', was growing, then it would somehow have to be diminished. If the children were to be *de*socialised as Aborigines and *re*socialised as whites, they would have to be removed from their parents.

Thus to the first rationale of separation, a hundred years old and underpinned by the ambience of selfless missionary endeavour, was added the second, that it was in the interests of the state, as well as of the children themselves, that they be removed from their communities and raised as white. Child removal, or to put it politically, the separation of the teaching generation from the learning generation, was seized upon as one administrative tool of a policy of dispersal, for it was much easier to whisk the children away into inaccessible places than to disperse a camp of a hundred adults who had nowhere to go. By 1910 it was politically less important that Aboriginal children become carpenters or maids. The vital purpose to the New South Wales administration was that, whatever else the children grew up to be, they should not be allowed to grow up as identifying Aborigines.

Should this seem rather unbelievable, it is as well to realise that social engineering projects of the 'save the child' variety were relatively common in an era when the state was beginning to take over all kinds of functions which it had previously left to enthusiastic amateurs. In Britain, city orphans (or so they were described) were often sent to the country, or overseas. New classes of 'deviance', which in retrospect seems to have been invented more to save private property than children, appeared in American and British statute books at the same time that Aboriginality itself was, as it were, discovered to be a deviance.

Little by little, child removal became a fundamental plank in the agenda of the Aborigines Protection Board. The argument rested on the supposed 'idleness and immorality' of the reserves from which the children would somehow have to be 'protected'. A long-time official of the Board told the Australasian Catholic Congress in 1909:

> We have to-day 3,200 children growing up in our midst, three-fourths of whom range from half-castes to almost white, with no prospects ahead of the great majority, under the present system, but lives of idleness and vice . . . under the evil influences and bad examples of the adults, they almost invariably drift into an aimless, useless life of idleness and immorality . . . For adults we can only make their track as smooth as possible—they will soon pass away; but the children require our gravest consideration . . . Amongst all those who have had large experience with the aborigines, and who take a deep interest in their welfare, there is no difference of opinion as to the only solution of this great problem,—the removal of the children and their complete isolation from

> the influences of the camps. Under no circumstances whatever should the boys and girls be allowed to return to the camps, except on a short visit in an emergency, and then only by consent of the department . . . In the course of a few years there will be no need for the camps and stations; the old people will have passed away, and their progeny will be absorbed in the industrial classes of the country.

'Their progeny will be absorbed': that was the root of the state's intentions. Two years after the passing of the 1909 Aborigines Protection Act the policy was made perfectly plain in the Annual Report:

> The Board recognise that the only chance these children have is to be taken away from their present environment and properly trained by earnest workers before being apprenticed out, and after having once left the aborigines' reserves they should never be allowed to return to them permanently.

In 1916 the Act was amended so that 'The Board may assume full custody and control of the child of any aborigine, if after due enquiry it is satisfied that such a course is in the interests of the moral or physical welfare of the child'. This gave officials the power to remove any child under any pretext, for not even a court hearing was necessary. From that time the Board's officers were at work removing hundreds of children—1500 by 1934—from the camps to which they were never to return. To this day their progress around the state can be traced by the numbers of children removed, in successive months at successive towns, throughout New South Wales. Two or three people in this book were removed under this section of the Act. They grew up in institutions, sometimes wondering why their mothers didn't keep them, never dreaming that no parent could possibly have saved their children from the relentless provisions of the 1916 Amendment once the Board decided to take them.

By 1939 a new Child Welfare Act relating to all the state's children caused this section of the Aborigines Protection Act to fall into disuse, even though it remained on the books until 1969. A court hearing became the norm although, as in Jean Carter's case recounted here, it was often a formality. But by 1940 it didn't really matter. So deeply entrenched were negative attitudes towards Aboriginality that to the whites separation seemed preferable to almost any divergence from the European nuclear family model. On the missions, welfare officers had instructions to send any children light enough to pass as white to the ordinary child welfare Homes, not the Aboriginal Homes, presumably in the hope that they would never know that they were Aboriginal. Difficult as it was for any unmarried mother to keep a baby born in a big public hospital, it became virtually impossible for an Aboriginal single mother. Almost all the mothers who have come to Link-Up in search of children adopted long ago speak of the irresistable pressures placed upon them to have their children adopted. Their stories are not included here, for this is a book about homecomings; their children have not come home because they have not yet been found.

By the 1950s, considerations of cost and new psychological theories which stressed the importance of the mother-child bond began to work against the Aboriginal Homes at Cootamundra and Kinchela. At the time when we might have expected a reduction in the number of separations, the statistics remained steady. The reason was the assimilation policy, officially in force throughout the Commonwealth, stated that every Aborigine should (or in a later version, would want to) adopt the lifestyle, habits and thinking of white people. A baby placed with white parents would obviously be more quickly assimilated than one placed with black parents. So ran official thinking, but more importantly, so also ran the feelings of the majority of honest and conscientious white citizens. The popular image of Aboriginality was a run-down camp, devoid of truly Aboriginal culture, overrun with children and dogs. Drunks, broken windows, dirt, disease. Even those who blamed the government for the squalor thought it still might be best that the child, for its own sake, should grow up in a comfortable suburban home. Therefore Aboriginal babies were not placed with black Aboriginal foster or adopting parents, but with white.

The people in this book who describe their foster or adoptive care were born after 1950 when this conscientious (but misguided) commitment to social welfare had been added to the justifications of child removal. There were still a few child-snatchers employed by the Board, but they were on the 'missions', as the reserves were still known. Most of the children in this book were born in city hospitals and raised by white parents who were often applauded in the press for their public-spirited actions. The attitude of such parents towards their children covered a very wide spectrum indeed. Some did their best but, because of their own mental prison about the nature of Aboriginality, it was a best which fell far short of being good enough in their children's eyes. Some parents loved their adoptive children as passionately as parents can. Yet their children did not find their homecoming any easier. It seems that, while being loved as a child can help to make a better balanced adult, it does not make it any easier to become an *Aboriginal* adult. Nor did a loving upbringing ensure that the adult would be shielded from 'coon' or 'boong'. White society made very few concessions to black children raised among the whites.

Whatever their attitudes, substitute parents had to accept the prevailing view that Aboriginal children were to remain away from their community and culture as long as possible, preferably forever. Adopting parents were told to destroy any information they may have learned about their child's origins, so that they might never find out who they really were.

'Really were?' To the framers of the Adoption Act the phrase had no meaning. The Act implied that when the original identity ceased to exist legally, it ceased to exist in actuality. This legal fiction has caused much harm to European adoptees, but to Aboriginal children it has been devastating. For an Aboriginal identity can never be said to be lost while people know the simple fact that they are descended from an Aboriginal parent or grandparent. It was this realisation which brought Link-Up into existence and which sustains it today. After nine years of reunions, two things are clear: that large numbers of separated Aborigines want to find their real identity, and that an Aboriginal identity is recoverable.

'Reflections', the third section of this book, indicates just how difficult and lengthy a journey this is. So much has been lost, so much has to be unlearned, so much has to be relearned; there may be something which, whatever one's history and experience, can never be recovered. Whether the children were institutionalised in white or Aboriginal Homes, fostered or adopted, loved, hated or ignored, they shared in common the mental torment of not belonging in a society to which the Europeans had innocently, ignorantly or arrogantly assumed they would belong. For whether they would or would not, they could not belong. White society accepted the children but not the adults.

If Europeans one hundred years ago had accepted the right of Aboriginal parents to raise their children as they wished, and if, today, they realised that there is still no real equality for Aboriginal people in this country, this book would not have been necessary. Instead, another one hundred thousand people would be identifying as Aboriginal citizens of Australia.

Peter Read

Link Up

Link-Up (NSW) Aboriginal Corporation was established in 1980 to reunite Aboriginal adults who had been fostered, adopted or institutionalised as children. We are supported by grants from the federal and New South Wales governments. We are non profitmaking, and our membership, full-time staff and governing body is entirely composed of Aboriginal people who were separated from their families.

On a typical day we might receive two new requests for help. One might be from a mother whose daughter was adopted from a city hospital thirty years ago. Since under present New South Wales law no information can be released by the adopting agency (usually the Adoptions Branch, Department of Family and Community Services) we can offer no direct help. We ask the Adoptions Branch to check its Adopted Persons Register to see if the child has registered as wanting family contact. We also check a similar Register we keep ourselves. If the response is negative, we cannot immediately make contact with the daughter because, despite years of enquiries, reports and recommendations by dozens of interested parties, the legal position regarding the release of information is inflexible. In other states such as Victoria, adopted persons over eighteen can apply to find out their origins, but in New South Wales, where so many thousands of Aborigines lost their identities, we can only advise the mother to help us to get the law changed, not to give up. We'll also invite her to one of our weekend meetings at which, if she wishes, she will meet mothers who have already found their children, mothers still searching, children who have found their families and children still searching.

The second call might be from a former foster child in his twenties, who knows his family name and birthplace. Fostering (by which a child remains a state ward) allows the release of the natural identity, so the family's location will normally be known. If desired we will visit the caller's mother, wherever she is living, to find out her wishes. Almost always she will want to see her son as soon as possible. We inform the son and, if he wishes, arrange a meeting with his family. Some weeks or months later the meeting takes place, usually in the family home. If arranged by Link-Up, which most people prefer, we will take the person home, cover the costs, and if necessary talk the nights away; for these few days may well be the watershed between two personalities and two identities. The new 'Link-Upper' may want help or advice from other members of the Link-Up community or may, like some of the mothers still looking for their children, attend the meetings which are held every six months.

Coming Home

When we, the editors, thought about this book a few years ago, we weren't sure from which aspect we would write it. We decided to approach it from the point of view of the children who had been removed from their families because that part of Aboriginal history—what happened to the children while they were away—is still relatively unknown. The experience of many Aboriginal families ended when their child was taken away, when they waved goodbye at the station as the train pulled out, or as the truck or welfare car disappeared around the bend. They knew no more until many years later when their child, now an adult, turned up again. There's a vast emptiness there. We thought it important to record the experiences of those children, to find out what sort of things they went through, and how separation affected them. We divided the recordings into three parts: the experience of childhood; the experience of returning home; and the contributors' thoughts a few months or years after their return.

Our children were removed under the New South Wales Protection Board and child welfare systems. One race believed they knew what was best for another race whom they considered inferior. Therefore they took the children to make them like themselves. But there were alternatives. If it was impossible for the parents to look after the children, there were other relatives like aunts or grandparents who could have taken them. In many cases there was no need for the children to be taken for long. If really necessary, they could have gone to the institutions at Cootamundra or Kinchela for three or six months and then returned home when their parents got back on their feet. There are many cases of parents writing letters to the Aborigines Protection Board asking for the children back, and yet they weren't seen again for forty years, if ever.

Some children were adopted, others went through different types of institutions. To produce this book, we tried to gain a perspective on a range of different experiences. There are people who are still separated from the community because their grandmothers were removed sixty years ago. They are now the second or third generations coming home.

Some are unable to come home emotionally for different reasons. One reason is that some people haven't thought about their Aboriginality very much. They have reached the stage of thinking, 'Right, I want to get home, I want to meet family', because of curiosity; they haven't thought much further than that. It's not their fault: at school a lot of children were called names and had no come-back for it. Feeling ashamed, they gradually withdrew and denied their Aboriginality. All their experiences reinforced the idea that they were something to be ashamed of. Every Aboriginal person who has been raised by white people has known that to a greater or lesser degree. Other people in the book are further along the road towards working out why they were removed, and have come to terms not only with their own experiences, but also with those of their mother and family.

It makes no difference how you were removed. I don't believe it matters in the long run whether children were removed forcibly or were adopted or fostered, because by the time they come to Link-Up, they are all suffering the same, or very similar, after-effects. They have all lost the same kinds of things.

One important loss is their history. I don't mean history in the wide sense, but a sense of knowing who they are. They missed out on all the family bonding, all the childhood experiences that bind people together. They missed out on all the stories and the funny things that have happened. That's what I mean by history—their own personal history which is the bonding. Sometimes it takes many years to get that back, because you have to recreate, start having experiences with your relations so that you have something you can talk about together when you meet them again: swimming down at the river, cups of tea in the kitchen. When you first go home you have no shared background, and you have to start making it.

Coming home is a long process. People start off in different ways, but I guess the first thing is an urge which becomes so strong that eventually you have to find out who you are. It begins to take over everything; it's all you can think about, it's all you want to do. You know you can't get on with anything else in your life until you find out.

That's usually the stage at which people come to Link-Up and ask for help. Often they are really frightened: while we're searching for their families, a lot of people are terrified that they'll be rejected, that the family won't want to know them. But of course they do. Once at home, they can sit and hear their family's funny stories and gradually get around to the question that has been bothering them most: Why was I removed? Then there's probably a visit to camping spots, cemeteries or places which are important to the family.

One of the hardest things people coming home to their families for the first time have to learn is not to judge. They may have been raised in a middle-class white family and may be coming home to ways which are not those they have grown up with. For example, there may be a large number of people coming in and out of the house. These people may be introduced; then they will sit and not speak, not even seeming to look. This contrasts with the European way of introduction by eye contact and lots of conversation. If the 'Link-Uppers' start judging, they're going to miss out on all the things they are actually coming home to, the things they are longing for emotionally. They can miss out on subtle things like a grandfather or an uncle coming up and saying, 'Doesn't she look like Auntie when she was her age?' or hearing, 'There's always a bed here for you.' If they are so busy judging the house in which their family live because of the way they have been raised, they will miss out on the real things that make up the homecoming.

Because the first meeting with their family was so great, some people suddenly think, 'I'm Aboriginal, I finally know who I am.' But then they can become caught in divided loyalties: 'I'm Aboriginal, but what do I do about my white family who raised me?'. It becomes an emotional tug of war. Some people get to the stage where they actually reject their white family because they feel that's what they have to do now that they're Aboriginal. Others find that it's very hard to talk to their white friends because they can't comprehend what they've just been through and are going through. They feel so good that they don't understand why their friends can't see that there's a difference. But not only do the friends not understand, they often don't *want* the 'white' friend they knew to suddenly change into an Aboriginal person, and they are uneasy at the transformation. So for a while the Link-Up person may have no white friends to talk to. For some people it's a beginning, but temporarily at least it's an ending too. They find the only people who really sympathise are Aboriginal people, for they are the ones who've had their kids taken from them.

For white families who have raised Aboriginal children, it is possible to grow to understand the change, but it takes a lot of effort. Often there are many heartaches and ripping apart before parents can come to an understanding that what their child is doing is right, and to accept that this isn't, say, just their little Jenny any more, the child they love, but Jenny an Aboriginal woman. She has a history and a background they could never provide. They still love her and she's still their daughter, but they have to accept that she is becoming something other than the person they have known.

Link-Up's attitude to this emotional tug of war is that, as much as possible, we help people to keep the relationships they have had. It's not necessary to leave the family who raised you; it's possible to live with two families, having different relationships with them and loving both of them. It takes a lot of effort on everyone's part, but that's what we aim for. We feel that we'd be ripping someone into two to say, 'Okay, now you've found your Aboriginal family you've got to shut the door on thirty years of your life amongst white people', as if it no longer existed. That would be really destructive.

Perhaps there is a message here too for white people who didn't raise Aboriginal children. The idea is not just to read this book, put it down and say, 'My God, that's awful, I feel so guilty.' We'd like people to understand what one race did to another, basically what human beings did to others. It's too easy to say, 'We have no connection with what happened 200 years ago, why should we feel responsible?'. For this didn't happen 200 years ago; these people are alive now. It isn't a system which is dead, along with those who went through it. These people are alive, they're still suffering, they're still trying to get home. It's something that affects not only the families who have raised Aboriginal children. With all good intentions, with all the love they could provide, in the end it's we who have to pick up the pieces.

In this book we have presented the facts; these things happened. It is now up to white people to accept them. But there is no point in them whipping themselves and not taking the next step, for once they can accept the facts, they can begin to help. We'd like them to try to understand and then to ask themselves: 'What attitudes do we have, what attitudes can we change which are negative towards Aborigines? What can we do to change things in ourselves?'. That's a big step. They shouldn't rush off to help some Aboriginal organisation if they're going in with bad attitudes.

When you go home, you are setting out on two journeys. First is the physical journey which is sitting in a car and driving to meet long-lost relatives. The second journey may take a lot longer. By coming home you're not just coming home to your family, you're finally coming home to yourself, to the self that is your birthright. It's a coming home to the realisation of the person you really are, so that you can finally stand up and know inside: this is me.

Do you ever arrive? Some people say not, I think yes. Of course you'll still have some bad moments, experiences in your life that overcome you when you least expect them. For me there was always a fear of Aborigines, instilled as a child, which could suddenly come up and take me over. One minute I could be quite comfortable talking to some Koories, and the next my insides were screaming, 'Run, run.' It took everything I had to control it and stay there. Those fears are hard to get rid of. What counts in the end is that you know, yourself, that you're Aboriginal, and that you are happy and comfortable with it. If you don't know some Koori expressions, in the end it doesn't matter, because you can always ask and people will tell you. For me, that's not being Aboriginal. It's part of it, but there's more than that; if you get to the stage where you are happy with yourself as an Aborigine, and strong in yourself for that, then all the other things don't matter. It's the emotional part of you, the heart not the head, that gets you through all these times.

Link-Up people understand that there's a difference between coming home to your family and coming home to your Aboriginality. People can come home to their families and still not feel Aboriginal, in fact the second journey can take several years. And when the feeling does come, it can be brought out not just by your family encouraging you, but by mixing with the Koori community. You are on your way as a Koori, even though you may not physically go home very often, when 'the natural family' becomes 'my family', when 'them' becomes 'us'.

The Text

The accounts that follow are transcriptions of taped interviews with the contributors. As editors, we made as few changes as possible to the text, preserving the original manner of speaking. Some of the transcriptions had to be shortened, and the use of individuals' names in contexts likely to cause offence had also to be omitted. Then the texts were returned to the speakers for their own correction. Some chose to leave the edited version as it was; others preferred to substitute their original speaking style for a written style. This decision was left entirely to the contributors. The governing body of Link-Up, all of whom are 'Link-Uppers' themselves, then read and commented upon the manuscript before it was offered for publication.

Overall the recordings occupied some sixty hours of tape. In order to let the contributors have time to reflect on their homecomings, they were chosen from people who had been involved in Link-Up in its first few years. They represent only a small number of those who have sought the help of our organisation since 1980. In that time we have answered perhaps some 500 requests for help.

Coral Edwards

ONE

Growing up

Jean Carter

What are your earliest memories?

Living at Peakhurst, we used to call it Saltpan. I remember being pulled over by my dog and being cut as a little girl, and having to have stitches. I remember Dad always talking, and sitting round the fire, being warmed, and having him talking all the time, being taught some songs. One was called 'Cricketer Boobelay', I don't know whether that's an Aboriginal song, but I used to sing it all the time, in me mind, when I was by myself. I must have been really pretty young then. I can remember Ruthy or Tommy, they were younger than me, but I don't remember one or two of my older brothers. I remember being brought home from the hospital. I must have been in hospital, 'cause Mum bought new socks for me and new shoes. Whether that was coming home from the hospital, or moving out to La Perouse, I just can't remember the change. I remember we used to go down at night, I remember seeing all the crabholes round the Georges River there. I remember older people being there in the background. I remember this big hill, always going up or down it.

I don't remember moving from there, but when we were at La Perouse—I can't even remember how long I was there, but we moved on that corner block. I remember we used to sleep outside the house, and I remember Chicka, one of my older brothers, and my eldest brother, Sago (Robert, named after Dad). I don't remember Sally very much, my sister, but I [by this time] remember Ruthy and Andy. Andy I was more close to, because we were going to school. Ruthy was in a younger class, she was a bit of a kid. But I remember Tommy, the baby, just crawling. I've got a good memory of him. I remember being in kindergarten—the teacher was red-headed; and going past Lapa [La Perouse] now, I can always remember the coral trees right near the infants class. We used to have the drill, air-raid shelter. They'd blow the siren, and you'd all have to run to this air-raid shelter, and I can remember standing in this big tunnel there until a certain time and we'd all have to come out. After school we used to just play round the mission with the kids, going to the beach. Mum used to take us round the rocks a lot.

Most of the time I can remember being in the bush getting five-corners, lilli-pillis, or down the beach. We used to get up really early in the morning with Mum and we used to go into the bush, she'd open up these little sugar bags, and make a little handle, and pick this little bush when the dew was still on it, lay the gum leaves one way, and the other green ferns the other, pack it in the bag. I still hear that crispy sound, you know. We used to walk round the houses, white people's houses and sell the little bunches of these things. Wasn't much around. I used to love condensed milk, that was a real luxury to have peanut butter. Those two foods were me favourites. My auntie, we used to go over to her place a fair bit, that was my father's sister. And one of my cousins, Joycie, and Norman, and Margie, she was the real pretty one. The old lady was very strict, I used to notice that. The eldest were the ones I remembered when I came back, back to Lapa.

Can you tell us what happened on the day you were taken?

Can't remember, sort of all blank. It was either the week before, can't think of the time, my brother went over to the Catholic school. I went over the next day, and I might have stayed half a week but when I saw the nun with a big strap, I was glad to go back to me class. And I always thought that was the reason why were taken. We were really frightened of those nuns with their big leather straps, and I used to think, it must have been because we went to that Catholic school. I just remember coming home, and Mum was at the door, and there was this car on the road outside. There was this white woman standing there, and I can hear mum saying, 'Can't you give me time to get the kids ready?'. And she said, 'No, they've got to go now', something like that. One minute we was comin' home to the house, and the next instant we was in the car and gone. I can't remember whether Tommy, who was just a baby, was in the car, I just know we were whisked away really quickly and there was only Mum there. We were never ever told why we were taken.

Next thing I remember we were in this place, it was a shelter sort of thing, and this big bath, huge bath, in the middle of the room, and all the smell of disinfectant, getting me hair cut, and getting this really scalding hot bath. Then putting on this big nightie thing, and I can't remember whether Ruthy was there, or Tommy. I don't know how long we was in that place, it was in Bidura, which is a [state government children's] shelter I think, in Glebe. I know it was Bidura, because I've been back there and . . . well I just freaked out when I went back there.

We must have been there a while, because I remember making a puppet there, and they had a little show, and I remember learning that song 'The Raggle Taggle Gypsies O'. Then one day, we were in this court house. I remember sitting outside, and Ruthy was with me, and I hadn't seen my brother or heard him since that day we left Lapa. And I could hear me brother in the court room, and he must've been only twelve or thirteen, and I could hear him saying, 'I'll look after the kids, sir. Just let us go home.' He was begging for his life. Our lives. He said something about 'I'll go to work.' And I didn't see him then till I came to Wreck Bay, and I was twenty-one then.

Did you ever find out if your parents were allowed in court that day?

No, we never ever saw Mum and Dad.

Did you ever find out why you were taken?

No. Never ever told.

Then I remember being taken down to this place where there was all these clothes. I remember getting fitted out,

I've never seen so many dresses, so many shoes. And I can't even remember the trip to Cootamundra [Aboriginal Girls' Home, run by the Aborigines Welfare Board]. The last memory of being in that place was being fitted out.

I can't remember travelling to Cootamundra, but I can remember the first day there. I knew I was a long way from home. I never saw scenery like that, mountains all round, all this dry country, and no water, no sea. That was one of the things I really missed.

[One day] I was playing and my sister wanted to go down the slippery dip. Ruthy was at the top, and one of the girls was at the bottom, and she wouldn't let her slide down. And Ruthy started to cry. All the kids was watching us, and anyway, I walked up to her, and I said, 'My sister wants to go down that slippery dip', and she said, 'Oh yeah?'. Something like that, 'What of it?'. Next minute she hauled off and punched me fair in the nose, and we started fighting. One of the grown-ups come down and I think we got punished for fighting or something. I thought it was really unfair.

There was this long driveway, and I always used to expect Mum and Dad to come up that driveway, always . . . I'd hear the train, and I'd think they might be on that. I remember Dad used to write, or maybe he just wrote the one letter. But I know I had the one letter, I used to read it every night. You know we used to have this little box under our bed with all our treasures, and I think I read that letter till it just crumbled up. I used to cry after I read it.

I used to write home. I always used to say, how long are we going to be here, when are you coming to get us, those sort of things. But I don't ever remember getting a letter from Mum.

There was a little school in the grounds, and I used to think, this schoolwork's really easy. And I went through all the grades that was there, but I still had to repeat this class for two years, and that's when they moved us down to sixth class down in the [local primary] school in Coota. Matron had got the girls to go down there. We used to have physical education at the Home, do all sorts of exercises with broom handles. And we used to do tap-dancing, used to get the Sunshine milk tins, flatten them down and make two holes each side and thread the elastic through so it would go over the top of your foot, and you'd put these little tins on for tap dancing. We used to do these little routines. Chocolates were real treats.

Then I started getting letters from Andy, and he always put a drawing in it. Andy's memory was always real clear in my head all the time, and we were close in age, I guess, I remember him more than Tommy. My world was then just Ruthy, me and Andy. Like, family. And I remember Mum and Dad, and I knew I had a sister Sally, but her memory was getting really faint. Tommy's memory got really dim, the baby brother.

I don't think I ever looked into the future. I knew that the girls were leaving at a certain age, and by this time I think I didn't mind Cootamundra then. Must've felt like home or something. I wasn't just in the Home routine then, because I was going to Cootamundra High School, and I had opportunities to go to other towns. But I used to wonder what it was like, you know, to go into somebody's home, 'cause my girlfriends were girls from the town, really good friends, we used to share lunches and things like that. I liked school and was really good at sports, and had an opportunity to go and run for the school.

Do you remember anyone telling you that you shouldn't ever go home?

I only remember the matron. I used to like her. She was strict and that, but she showed me a bit more concern than the others. But she used to say things to me that would make you feel a little bit down. Mum did come up and see us, once, and she was camped over in the cemetery. She wasn't offered any room there, wasn't welcome, she was allowed to stay [only] during the day, and I remember another girl whose mother came and sorta came up the next day. Just something like, 'Oh, your mother shouldn't be sleeping round in a cemetery', something like that. That sorta made me real . . . ashamed of Mum, but still a bit cranky with her for saying it. But then it made me think, 'Oh, maybe Mum *shouldn't* be sleeping in a cemetery.'

I remember Mum came, she had this big bag of ribbons, these lovely hankies all ironed and that, stacks and stacks of hankies and ribbons, all washed and ironed. I remember running down the road when I saw her coming, she was right down the end of the drive. And when I got to her I propped, you know. I was running and crying, I was running towards her. And when I got near her I propped, you know. Sort of stopped. Froze or whatever. I said, 'Mum, you've been drinking.' She said, 'No, baby, I haven't.'

I was a cruel kid, I was. That's what I find it hard to forgive meself for saying those sort of things, ask those sort of questions because . . . Cootamundra can be freezing at that time of the year. Probably sleeping out in the cold in the cemetery, trying to sleep. Just because I saw her with red eyes I asked her had she been drinking. That's the first words I said. I'd seen her drinking [at La Perouse]. I never ever saw her drunk, but I remember her drinking. My memory is that she never drank, and then, just one day, that sorta changed. I don't know that I ever saw her drink, just knew she'd been drinking.

Did someone on the staff tell you she was a drinker?

See Mrs Healy and Mrs English [the Board's child welfare officers, not attached to the Cootamundra Home] used to have these real confidential talks with me, 'cause I think I used to rely on them to get me information about my parents, about home and that, and I must have asked them. 'Cause I used to try and get them by themselves. I'd want to get them aside and just vaguely remember them saying little things like that, about family. They were more or less on the outside world. I think she was the one told me when Dad died, and Mum died. It was Mrs English each time. I don't know, I used to cling to Mrs English a bit, she didn't talk really harshly like the staff, she had a softer sort of tone.

Was that the only time your mother came?

Yeah. She stayed a week, I was about twelve or thirteen. When I was in first year there must have been this thing about alcohol in the Home, I signed a pledge when I was fourteen never to drink.

Were there other attitudes which you picked up there?

Well the first time I realised, I guess, that I was different, was at High School. I was in one of the classes, I was class captain. We used to have this book, secretary would write out the minutes, you know, and there was one of the boys, I forget his name, and he used to always draw. Anyhow, he drew this drawing, and I never saw it. And I could hear the kids laughing, and saying, 'Oh you shouldn't have done that,' really annoyed with him. When I came back I wanted to look at the minutes, look at this drawing. I never saw it, but I felt that it was something about being an Aboriginal. I was real hurt, the feeling was pretty strong that it was something. I couldn't stand him after that. And we were encouraged to study. Matron Hiscocks, she was really good like that. But your family, you know, there was just sorta like a vacuum around you really, your feelings and that. When we'd have Australian history I used to cringe, I used to hate going back to class, 'cause they'd be talking about Aborigines being primitive and savages, things like that. I used to get really angry about that description. I knew I was Aboriginal, but my personality or identity wasn't as strong as it is now. I was the second Aboriginal girl to go through High School, so there was that thing about being Aboriginal. Then there was that thing about getting the Intermediate Certificate, not many Aboriginal kids got that.

Did you want to go home as soon as you left Cootamundra?

No. Come to think of it, I was at Cronulla, came down, I knew that La Perouse was round there, but there was none of my family there. If Mum and Dad was there it would have been different. I wanted to see La Perouse but I was too—I don't know, scared I think, to go back. I was seventeen. I used to wonder how far away it was. During my early time at Coota one of the girls kept running away, and got bashed by the staff; there was a couple of the girls caught. I used to think, I couldn't go, because I had Ruthy, and had to think of her. I was sorta expecting me parents to come and get me, and the years went by. Well, I went down to Cronulla, and was there two weeks. I was working at Young, they came down for the holidays, and I couldn't move, because I was looking after their three kids. Well I made friends with the girl, and the son of the owner of the holiday cottage, and they asked me to go to the pictures, or come down to the beach, but I couldn't go, I was minding the kids. They said something to their mother, and she rang Mrs English, and they came down and told me to pack me things, and took me and that's when I came to Ashfield to work in the nursing home there. Well I knew La Perouse was round that next corner, but I knew Mum and Dad weren't there.

I was working at Ashfield, in a private nursing home, and there was other Koori girls there from the Territory, and we used to go out for the day, down to Manly, over to the zoo or the botanical gardens. Then one day I went for an interview with some hospital in Zetland. I was going to start training there, but they said I had to be eighteen, and I wasn't eighteen, so one day Mrs English said I could start in Victoria, Maroopna Base Hospital, you could be seventeen. I was just thinking—when I was in Coota I always thought I'd go back to La Perouse, and on my days off at Ashfield I wouldn't go out there. Something happened there. I always thought that I'd let the Home down, or something [if I returned].

Did you finish your training at Maroopna?

No I didn't finish training. I met my son James' father, and did have the opportunity to finish, but I was always afraid that welfare would take him. Anyhow, the nurses and sisters, we were all really good mates. They said, 'You're pregnant Jean.' I said, 'No.' They said, 'We can give you something.' I said no, so I worked, you couldn't even see I was pregnant, I was really flat and trim, about a week before I had James. Mrs Healey saying, 'Are you sure you're pregnant Jean?'. I said, 'Oh, yeah.'

Shortly before the birth of James, Jean moved back to Crown St Hospital, in Sydney.

About a fortnight after I finished down there I had James. There was a new Australian lady next to me in the ward and she'd lost her baby or something and she wanted James. I had a bit of pressure on me from the staff, they said she's got a beautiful home and that, it would be good if they could take James. Even the father came over and started talking to me. And I got real . . . I wouldn't let him out of me sight, James. [In Crown St] I had an opportunity to go back to nursing, but I was frightened they were going to take him. Sal used to mind him, I used to work—scrub floors, cleaning stoves, all that stuff, wash. I bought him a little three-wheeler bike, and I'd get on the back with him.

STAN BOWDEN

What is your earliest memory?

I think going from Bomaderry [Home for Aboriginal children run by United Aborigines Mission] to Kinchela [Home for Aboriginal boys run by Aborigines Welfare Board]. On the train. There was another bloke, Ian Harris,

Stan Bowden, aged 12

who had irons on his legs, and meself, and there was a woman. I was about ten. I didn't know where I was going, or why. Just that there was this old woman, Mrs Higgins, on the train, she took him and I up.

Just that . . .

Could you give an idea of a typical day at Kinchela?

Well you had a roster which lasted a month, I think it was. Different things you had to do, in the kitchen, or out in the yards, toilets, bathrooms, cleanin' up the dormitories, and each month it was changed over. Whatever you had to do in the morning you did before you got ready for school. You had to get it all done before. [The first thing was that] one of the staff came and called yous, wash and clean yourself up and that, then go out and do your work, then come back and ready for school. Some jobs you continued on after school, like farming, laundry and cleaning up yards and that. We had tea roundabout five, then if there was light you'd go out and play a bit more, then you'd go to bed and that. You had to lean up near your bed and say your prayers. Went to bed. There is a lot of things you can't talk about to anybody else. I can't even put it to words . . .

Kinchela Home for Aboriginal Boys, 1955

How old were you when you were put out to work?

I'd just turned fifteen. I went to school there but I wasn't good on a lot of subjects, and each year, at the show in Kempsey, and the school wanted to be represented by different things that was made at the Homes. They found out that I was good at weaving baskets, but a lot of things like spelling and all this, that I wasn't good at, when the spelling come, they just sent me out for makin' baskets for the shows each year.

Can you remember the managers?

I can only remember the one. He treated me different from a lot of other boys. I mixed with his kids. Not actually mix, but if he was goin' anywhere, he'd leave me to sort of, to babysit his kids when he went out. So a lot of time I was up at his place. Sometimes at night.

Who were your mates?

Well the ones I can remember were Ian Harris, that I went with from Bomaderry. Gordon [Edwards] I got on really well with, he was as much a brother as Cecil.

Did you know anything about your brothers and sisters?

I think I found out I had another brother, Alec, and a sister Florence. I didn't know about other brothers and sisters till after I left the Home. Alec came up a couple of times to visit—he was in before my time. Cecil was in there, and he was there when I left. 'Cause he went on to High School, which I never. Somebody mentioned that he was my brother, and Cecil mentioned Alec, and sister Flo.

PAULINE MCLEOD

How old were you when you were separated from your natural family?

Two years old originally, and when I was four years old I went to Muda and Papa [adoptive parents]. [Before that] I was placed in many various foster homes and institutions. I had two sets of foster homes, and apparently I was picked up in an institution of some sort. The story we were told that, being very religious people, Muda was quite sick when she was young, and when they had come over from Europe—it was just after the war—and racism against European people was very much there. She got quite sick, and she knew the plight Aboriginal people were facing, or had a slight understanding. She thought she was going at one stage, and made a pact with God, saying that if you allow me to live I'll look after children who really do need families. That's how it all occurred. I was the eldest among the [adopted] family. After me was another girl younger than myself, then a number of boys.

What did your foster parents think about Koories?

Very similar to most white people, which is: Aboriginals are drunk, they don't work hard, they go walkabout, they never seem to achieve much. Sometimes it was because the way things were, sometimes because they chose it. We weren't never to be like that: we were different. We were the lucky ones, chosen to help our people. That's why we had been given the opportunity to live with them. [We were told this] all the time. And to me it was important to be accepted into a family. I've always known that. It was always the greatest fear that if I didn't fit in, that I would be taken away. There was always that great fear. I'd think, 'I've lost one family, I don't want to lose another', so I'd always do whatever they'd say. Even things that were quite hurtful or annoying, I'd take it.

Can you remember when you became aware that you were Aboriginal?

I hanged around with a young girl who almost certainly had cerebral palsy. She couldn't walk properly, couldn't talk properly, she and I were the best of mates. I think then I noticed not so much that I was Aboriginal but that I was different. The real memory of being Aboriginal occurred when I was nine years old. We'd moved to a different school, and the kids asked us to eat witchetty grubs. Then it was quite obvious to me that I was Aboriginal. We were the first Aboriginal kids they'd ever had in this little country school. Then the eldest of us [Pauline] had to be the one to make sure we weren't picked on, that we upheld the honour of the Schmidt [adoptive] family, and no one would walk all over us. So we literally had to fight for our rights in the school. I'd have to make sure that everything was calm, or fight on behalf of the family members that were picked on.

The Schmidts were from Europe and they were very much the outsiders as well in the community, everywhere we lived. Our family just kept very much to ourselves. We never mixed with any groups when I was a kid. We were just basically brought up by ourselves. No one was allowed to call us names, poke fun of us. We were Schmidts and Schmidts weren't allowed to let that kind of thing happen to them. You had to fight, and we were really brought up fighting. I understand that when we came home crying and upset, Muda would sit down and say, 'Yeah look, you are different, yes you have got coloured skin and you should be proud of it. One day my freckles will join together and I'll be just the same as you.' Apparently that would calm us, we'd be quite happy then.

We spoke a lot of their language at home, and to decipher English from this language sometimes was quite difficult. I was a fluent speaker of their language then, and really got to know their culture. The [Child Welfare] Department thought it was great, that we fitted in so well as a family.

A [Child Welfare] officer heard it and expressed his delight in the fact. And we dressed up in traditional costumes at a fancy dress, traditional music. In Church at Christmas time we would sing in their language. We were very much orientated and brought up in their tradition and ways. So it was difficult to understand the Australian culture, let alone the Aboriginal culture. The first real Australian meal I ever had was when I was in High School and went on a hockey excursion and was billeted in an Australian home. Gravy, steak, mashed potatoes, peas, an apple and custard pie. Oh, what's this? Just incredible! Fascinating! I thought it was great. I loved it. I got to see what an Australian family looked like and acted.

What had you been told about your natural family?

I was told that they'd abused me, and that because of that abuse I was taken away, and that if they really cared or really loved us, they would have contacted us. This was up till I was twelve, and then it stopped. I never asked again.

A lot of things happened, a lot of things within the family. In that year [when Pauline was about twelve] I met Rachel [natural sister]. Went to High School. Also Muda was quite ill in hospital, she had gallstones and a heart problem. Anna [older natural child of Muda and Papa] was away at college. Papa was looking after us. He also—I don't know if it was rape or what—Sally and I shared a room. In the middle of the night I'd wake up and he was on top of Sally. I was scared witless. I never said a word because I was scared he'd do it to me. I remember waking up in the middle of the night and hearing him say to Sally, 'Don't you ever say a word', whispering. Fearful. Total fear. I don't know if he ever came to me, I think when he was bored with Sally he came to me.

He approached me once. He called me into the room. I was a happy-go-lucky person at that stage, didn't occur to me what was going to happen. I was more interested in climbing trees and looking after animals and things. And he kissed me, and I almost fainted. I thought, 'How disgusting.' He then showed me his private parts and I almost vomited. I thought it was the ugliest sight I ever saw. Then he told me to lie down on the bed. And wait for him. I just almost . . . I was ready to jump through the window. I think he knew that. So he just stopped and said if you ever say anything to anyone that he'd kill the rest of us. And I got up.

Can't tell anyone. Never did. Never did. First time ever.

And he never went any further. So I never, ever . . . I hated the idea. Of any relationship with men.

And your mother never knew?

No. If she did, she never said anything. But I don't think she ever knew. I don't know how I felt, to be honest. If I would've been able to, I would've forgotten about the whole thing. But I can't. And I just don't know really how I felt at that time. All I knew is, I was feeling quite sick. And I hated fellers. It just helped me stay within the library at school, and not mix in with people.

[Now] I think of him as my father and look for excuses for him. Say he was sick at the time.

What else happened in that year?

I had rheumatic fever when I was twelve, and was in hospital in September/October/November, and then when I was thirteen I had moved from Primary to High School and I was away from the rest of the family. Literally, this was my first time. And I really wasn't mixing with people. I was really the outsider.

Our family was quite poor. [Once I was asked] if I would go down and buy something for this girl. I thought it was a good way to make friends so I did it. Also she said, if I wanted anything else, to book it up as well, while I was booking her things. So I went overboard, I booked about $24 worth of things in the space of about four months, and got myself in quite a lot of hot water over that. Real trouble, because it was considered stealing, and that was a great no-no in our family, to even think of doing that. And I had really made the big botch. And I lied through my teeth. I would not admit that I had done the wrong thing. I was scared witless that I was going to be removed. It was actually said that if I didn't tell the truth I would be removed, or taken away. Out of fear, I had taken a gun and shot myself. 'Cause I just didn't want to go into a Home.

While I was in hospital recovering from the shot, I was told by Muda that if I ever said anything wrong, I wouldn't be allowed back with them. Even after I had shot myself. So I lied through my teeth. The child psychologist or whatever she was, when she came along, I said, 'Rosy red', everything was all right, nothing was wrong. And it worked. I told the welfare that I had shot myself because I was scared I was going to lose them, and that Papa had said if I didn't tell the truth I couldn't return home. It wasn't so much the truth. I had no intention of going to a Home, if they were going to take me to a Home they would drag me. So once again, if I wanted to stay in the family, I had to lie through my teeth and get back into everybody's favour. And I did that, quite successfully.

How did you feel about being Aboriginal in High School?

I suddenly found myself at High School by myself, and

once again the only Aboriginal person, and I found it quite difficult to cope. Now I realise the greatest fear was that if I didn't fit in, I would be taken away. And I really became a person that just didn't mix with anyone whatsoever. I spent my time in the library reading and not going out in the playground. If I could I'd find myself in the library or in fantasyland, imagining things. In High School I never had a friend. Didn't want a friend, my whole life was in the family. Whatever I did was wholly and solely for the family, trying to please Muda. Trying to be the good example for others to follow. It became very important for me to be the big sister, the example. And that the part of the structure of the family, the eldest was the example and took the responsibility if anything went wrong.

I started to realise about Aboriginal culture and my own Aboriginality when I was about fifteen. There were more Aboriginal people around the place, and Muda and Papa had decided it was about time we started mixing with Aboriginal culture. We'd gone to meetings through the AECG [Aboriginal Educational Consultative Group], I started getting a cheque each fortnight through the Aboriginal Study Grants, a lot of books.

I still don't know why I couldn't [stay on at school], even to this day I can't figure out why. They said to me—I was extremely moody, depressed a lot, quite angry with everyone. I'd sit there and say, 'I want to go on', and they'd say, 'No you're not.' But I went to tech and did ticket-writing. I liked that because I've got an artistic flair as well. Then I went back to school again, did fourth form. I did my School Certificate and then wanting to go on, but I was told no. Once again, apparently, it was too much for me. I desired to do it so bad but I was told no.

Also, Rachel, my oldest sister, had attempted contact. I went and saw her. I was really muddled, and I can't remember anything that occurred. I was scared of meeting her, I was scared I was going to lose the family I had—they didn't like the idea of me meeting Rachel. In my excitement I had this fantasy picture of Rachel: she was going to be beautiful, everything was going to be great. And Rachel wasn't when I met her. She was really what I know now as a streetwise person. She knew how to survive out in the world, totally different from me. Because of our own different stages, she never appealed to me, and Muda and Papa didn't encourage too much contact or too much follow up. Instead of saying, 'Go ahead, you should write', they'd say, 'It's all right if you don't.' Eventually the contact was lost with Rachel.

After leaving school Pauline worked as a nursing assistant at a local hospital for a short time. She then worked in various community groups and found that she was interested in the welfare field.

That was when I started to realise about my Aboriginality. Got into college, two years at college, and did my Associate Diploma [in Welfare Studies], studied up about Aboriginality, got involved in a lot of groups, AECG, really started to speak up that year. Most of my topics were on Aboriginal people and problems they faced in the past, the whole history of the Aboriginal culture and community. I checked into health, education, welfare, touched on prisons, did a stint in various community groups and found out how much I really liked to work there.

After a term in Armidale as a trainee Aboriginal District Officer in the Department of Youth and Community Services, Pauline transferred as an ADO in the Hunter region.

I had a few problems with the ADOs in the Hunter. I never figured out why, what it was, that made me different from them. I mean, I tried to do the right thing, I tried to explain what I knew about Aboriginal issues, Aboriginal people and what I had learned, but it never seemed to get anywhere. And once again it was a great isolation thing. I was different from the rest of them. I had a good fight with one, I got quite upset with him because he was an Aboriginal feller, he was fighting against me as a District Officer, saying 'You're white establishment, you're raised by white people, you wouldn't understand the black kids that were placed in a Home', things like that. I found out that I was fighting for my own identity, to be accepted by Aboriginal people. No matter what I did, it still wasn't enough, I wasn't accepted as an Aboriginal person by the Aboriginal people! And that almost was the last crunch. There were times when I really thought I was going to suicide. Because I wasn't fitting in anywhere. I just wasn't fitting in to any community whatsoever.

As a welfare officer, were you able to get hold of your own file?

I didn't trust anyone with my feelings. Every now and then when I tried, someone used it and abused it against me. Always happened that way. So after speaking to this RDO [Regional District Officer] she organised it so I received my file from down in Central Office, which came about a couple of weeks later. I read it in a rush, I had to quickly read as much as I could. In that time I wrote down the names of the members of my [natural] family, their dates of birth, last known addresses, from Mum, Dad, Rachel, Michael and Rodney, and write down as much information as I could about my medical history, especially my younger years, to try to figure out who the heck abused me. When I was a child, somewhere along the line I was abused. I've got a beaut scar right across the arm here. I was told it happened because I was abused. I've also got a scar here and a skin graft all over here. Also I wasn't the brightest person under the sun, and I was told I was abused on the head and was in a children's home for the mentally handicapped. I can remember sitting in the sun for hours learning how to spell 'Australia'. I was told that it was the natural family that did it. And Muda and Papa couldn't tell me who it was, the mother or the father—but one of them did.

Also in that particular file it said I had been taken away because we had no fixed place of abode. Totally contradicting what Muda and Papa had told me, what I'd been told and believed all these years. It takes me a while for things to sink in, and it took me a while for that to sink in. I was working, and I was trying to get something organised in the Aboriginal community and I found out that the RDO was using the information against me. Once again I fell into the trap of trusting a person.

I was having a heck of a time at home and I was constantly thinking about my natural family. Things weren't clicking. Things I had read in my file just didn't fit with what I had been told. Things were just getting too much for me . . .

That's when I decided really to start looking for my natural family.

NEVER MORE

Separated
Fretting, sad.
Given into other hands.

Parents, sister, brothers gone.
Wondering what did
I do wrong!?!

Institution big and cold
All this happen
when one year old

Confused and lost
I didn't know
That the Government decreed it so.

Different places
till five year old
Then went to family
as I was told.

(Going once . . . Going twice!
Sold!
To that lovely couple
Who's not too old . . .)

So that is how it all began
Simply taken from
My home and land.
Who would lift an eye today
After all it didn't happen yesterday!
But remnants of the child's cry
Echo loud in my mind.
As I feel the inner fear
Of rejection, injustice coming near.
A victim of circumstance
I must fight, my life to enhance.
To be totally free of it all
I must live through it once more.
For my spirit and culture to be as one
I must go back to where it all begun.
The child of one must be taken in hand
And shown through her ancestral land.
Where the old people will heal her heart
As her culture she becomes a part.
Never more to be taken away
As it had happened in her younger day.
Make sure it never happens again
Please! No more, the hurt, the pain.

Sharon Carpenter

Have you always known you were Aboriginal?

No, I didn't know I was Aboriginal until I was about thirteen even though people at school used to ask me, and I used to say no—because I didn't know at that stage. It wasn't till one of my white aunties told me. But I always sort of felt it was there. I asked her actually, and she said 'Yes you have got a bit in you.' She said that my great-grandmother, one of her relations was Aboriginal, that she was the first Aboriginal woman to marry a white man in a church. But that's either all the info she knows or that she's going to tell me.

Sharon Carpenter at the time of the interview for *The Lost Children*

How did you feel?

Pretty excited. A confirmation of my feelings, basically. When I was growing up I never had any friends at school and I always used to feel really isolated. I used to come home crying and saying, 'Mum, why haven't I got any friends?'—just feeling different. I used to get called things like 'wog'—not 'Abo' or anything like that—but they knew I was different. And then Mum used to rub coconut oil on us and chuck us out in the sun, me and my sister. I used to go real brown, eh. My grandfather, my father's father, who's white, he used to freak out 'cause I was so brown you know. But it was a personal thing then. I feel differently about it now, I feel like I don't have to keep it to myself any more.

Could you explain how it all came about?

The only thing I know about my great-grandmother is

that one of her relations, I don't know who, was the first Aboriginal woman to marry a white man in a church. That's one side of my family. Then there's my mother's father. My mother was brought up by her grandparents. [My grandmother] ran and hid when she got pregnant 'cause she never married my mother's father. After she had Mum, she just left her to be brought up by her grandparents. I've been round to see her [grandmother] a few times now but she doesn't want to say. She's ashamed of it obviously, because her family's Catholic and to have a child out of wedlock in those days: big shame. She has just totally isolated herself from the family, she doesn't have anything to do with us. I asked her once, [i. e., Sharon's grandfather's identity] and she said, 'Yes, he was Aboriginal.' But then she denied it the second time when I wanted to know more. She just said, 'Did I say that?'. So it's pretty hard. There's no records or anything. It's all in the family. She's a very stubborn old woman.

I know [that she may never tell me]. I don't like thinking about that. That's a pretty horrible thought to me, the thought of going through the rest of my life not knowing my people. If I found out I'd just love to go to that place and just feel that these are my people, this is my land, you know that feeling? That's really important to me. To go through my life and now even know that—I don't even like to think about it. She's seventy-six now. She just says to me, 'It's my secret and I'll never tell anyone.' And it's really hard for me to go and visit her because she's like a stranger to me. To try to talk about something like that. She'll happily talk about the weather, but anything else . . . It's hard to talk to her about close things.

The feeling [of being Koori] got stronger as I got older. It got to the point where I wanted to meet other Aboriginal people and that became a pretty intense feeling. It was just like a magnet. Whenever I saw Aboriginal people I just wanted to go there. So that's what I did. My first feeling was when I used to live in Redfern in the high-rise flats which is just behind the Clifton, a real black pub in those days. Every Friday night I knew the blackfellers used to go there and I used to just look out my window and watch them going in, you know, I really wanted to go in there. It was a really strong feeling to go in there. I eventually did one night. I just walked in and sat down and just observed people, stayed there for about an hour. After that I just wanted to do more things, get to know more Aboriginal people and I suppose it sort of snowballed.

What was it like being there for that hour?

It was strange in a way because I didn't know anyone, but then again I felt relaxed. Even though I'd never do it now, but I wished that I knew some people so that I could talk to someone. I wouldn't do it now, I've realised a lot more things about Aboriginal people: if they don't know you when you go into a community, they're very wary of you. Now I would've done it differently. I would've tried to meet at least one person in the community that I could trust and then get them to introduce me to people. It was funny the first time I went down the mission in Redfern [i.e. Eveleigh Street region]. I still get funny feelings about going there when you've been away for a while. The first time I went down there it was just so different, you know, everyone was staring at me because they didn't know my face. I always had a fear that they thought I was white. I still have that fear with a lot of Koories that they think I'm white. Just being an outsider and not living there makes you sort of—I dunno—uncomfortable I suppose.

Did you go back to that pub again?

I think I stayed away for a little while because I was working at a theatre restaurant. Then I studied dance for a year and a half at the Aboriginal and Islander Dance Theatre at Glebe. After I left the Dance Theatre I had my son Wanjun. The next couple of years I spent mainly at home. By then I had a few Koori friends but it wasn't until I went to the Eora Centre [Aboriginal college of performing and visual arts] and met a lotta people from Redfern that I really got involved with the community.

Can you remember times when you were put down for not knowing where you came from?

Sometimes it's really strange, you know, that you can be really fair but that feeling of being Aboriginal is so strong. It's really difficult, it's really hard because you feel as black as they look, but you *don't* look like that so it's a real problem. And I realise now that maybe it's the young people in the community who put shit on you like that, it's not the older people, they understand you. I mean there's plenty of times when I've felt maybe I'm not Aboriginal, maybe they're right. But it's only been through old people saying—like there's this old lady from Mornington Island said, 'I can see Aboriginal in you, girl'—that was the thing that kept me going. What the old people think is important.

And then I was in the Clifton one day with this girl from the Dance Theatre and she knew a lotta people there and I didn't and this old feller was sitting next to me. And he was just looking at me and I never thought much about it. And he just came out and said, 'You know girl, if you sit on a fence one day you're going to fall off.' And that really stuck in my mind. That was about six years ago, but it wasn't till last year that I wrote a poem about it. It's really true, but that's how people make you feel. Blacks and whites. White people say, 'Oh you must be only one-eighth caste' and all this sorta stuff. I don't think I'll ever get right off the fence until I find out where I come from. Because you've always got some blacks saying to you, 'You don't know your family name, you don't know where you come from, how do you know you're Aboriginal?'

How do you answer them?

Well I have to explain my whole life story and that becomes a real hassle, and sometimes they think I'm making all of this up. It just becomes a real problem. I think it's easier if you've been adopted because straightaway they understand it. But if you're in circumstances like mine where it goes back three generations, and the possibility of Mum's father being Aboriginal, to explain all that sort of stuff: 'One of my great-great-relatives was one of the first Aboriginals to marry a white man in a church . . .' and all this. It's just such a hassle. It's just really difficult meeting other Aboriginal people. They say, 'G'day sis, where are you from?'. 'I dunno.' It's really horrible having to say that all the time. You just wanna be proud to say, 'Oh, I come from here or I come from there', just a simple thing like that. A lot of Aboriginal people don't understand. They take it for granted because they've known where they're from all their lives, and their family. It's really easy for them in that way.

Why are people like you rejected, do you think?

I think maybe it's because the Koories who have grown up in the cities and towns have had such a struggle, maybe they think, 'Oh you've grown up white and had it all easy and now you want the glory of being black.' I can understand that. But it has to be a two-way thing. They have to understand how we feel as well. We've got the choice to be black or white, that's what they don't realise. But if I was to live in a totally white environment all the time I'd always be thinking about my people and wanting to do things with them. I know I've always had those feelings, even when I was a child. It's always been there. I couldn't sit in a room full of whitefellers and them putting down blackfellers, pretending that I'm one of them. I couldn't do that, I'd get too angry. It's easy when white people say you're not black, that doesn't hurt. But when black people say you're not, that hurts. I can hack white people saying to me, 'Gee you don't look Aboriginal, you must be only an eighth', 'cause I can then say, 'Well if you'd been colonised for 200 years and your great-grandmothers had been raped, you'd look like me too—it's your fault

I look like this, not mine!', you can throw all that back at them. But for an Aboriginal person to say, 'You're not Aboriginal', that hurts. The main thing is that you have to get the Aboriginal communities to understand what Koories like us have been through, and that's what this book will do, I hope.

SITTING ON A FENCE

What's ya name sister?
Where ya from?
I don't know
Wishing I could say
Cowra, Moree or Tamworth
Like everyone else.

Identity crisis
Interrogation and pressure from black and white
Like it's my fault

Feeling the spirit in my soul
Stronger than blackness of skin
Or name or place
Missing link
How I wish I knew.

This feeling lives in strength,
Only those who have been there
Feel the insecurity,
The sadness,
The dream in life to know.

PAUL CREMEN

Mum was brought up in an orphanage. My grandmother died and left my mother in the charge of an orphanage, and Mum had a pretty rough trot there. She knew she was an Aborigine, but I don't think it was emphasised. It was just the fact that she knew, and that was it. Mum would've been three or four when her mother died. It was a Catholic place, in Lane Cove [Sydney], because Mum tried to find out some information and got as far as the door of the orphanage, and they wouldn't give her any information. I think the only thing she knew was her mother's Christian name, that was about all.

[My mother] was a number in the orphanage, I don't think she even got her real name. From what you found out, she was [called] Julia, but she was always brought up as Doreen. But I think she was more often called Josephine in the Home. But she did say that she was a number: maybe she meant she was treated as a number, instead of as a person. All I can ever remember her saying, was that she used to have a doll, and that doll became community property, and she was always upset about that. She always remembered that. Because Mum used to drink a bit and it used to come out when she was really upset. That was the only link she had with her mother, apparently, and she had that doll taken off her.

Mum was there from 1934, when she was about four, and my father tells me she was allowed out at sixteen. She was very naive, and knew nothing of the world at all, nothing at all, and she wasn't prepared for meeting people or anything. Apparently she had a job as a housekeeper of some description, and she had a couple of nasty incidents with a man there that she wasn't prepared for, knew nothing about. That put her off a little bit. [But] Mum always thought she came from Condobolin way—apparently she was told at the orphanage as a child that she came from back of that way.

So you always knew you were Aboriginal?

My mother told me I was. It wasn't foremost in my mind, it never worried me one way or the other. It wasn't some great revelation or anything. I just knew. I don't remember when I was told. Dad never mentioned it. Mum always got really happy when Yvonne Goolagong won Wimbledon, that was later on though. But I didn't go out of my way to speak to any of them, if anything, I avoided them more. 'Cause I didn't really know, so I didn't say anything. I didn't think I looked Aboriginal, I knew my father wasn't Aboriginal, and there wasn't a lot [of Aboriginal people] in Blacktown, where I was living. [As I grew up] I didn't chase anything [i.e., information] then. Mum told me all that she knew, and I didn't know there was any way of finding out. I could [only] go on what Mum told me.

I came down here [to Nowra] in 1982, and I was out of work for two and a half years. But this is the area where all the Aboriginals are, there's a lot of missions [i.e., reserves] round here, and when I was out of work and desperate, I thought I'd try and check out what was happening, you know. I thought they might be able to find out more about myself. So I went into the Cultural Centre and met Jane Ardler, [Co-ordinator of the South Coast Aboriginal Cultural Centre] and she said she'd get on to Coral [Edwards, Co-ordinator of Link-Up], to find out more about myself and my family. I remember telling her that my grandmother died in Newington State Hospital [Sydney] (because Mum found that out somehow) which was at the time like a nursing home, but it was for Aboriginals. And when I said that to Jane Ardler, a bloke there working with her said, 'That sounds about right because that's where they used to throw the old Aboriginals. Put them out.' Since then, it's been a mental hospital. Or was. If it was a mental hospital then, one can only assume that the eye affliction my grandmother had [which had caused her to be sent from Condobolin in Sydney in about 1928] had drove her to such a state that she needed to be there. So when I mentioned that, this bloke said, 'You *must* be Aboriginal.' Jane said she'd check out further, and she put me on to Coral.

How did you feel when you went into the Cultural Centre?

I'd been out of work for a long time, four kids to support,

and I thought well, if I'm Aboriginal, maybe someone can help me, make things a little bit easier. I didn't realise the things it was going to open up, that I was going to learn so much. I just went in to see if I could get some help. I thought, 'Aboriginals are getting everything, *so they reckon.* All the whites reckon Aboriginals are getting this and that for nothing.'

Could you have gone into a place like that ten years earlier?

No, but it was the fact that Mum had died; and when I wanted to know anything [earlier], Mum sorta . . . I had Mum to talk to, not that she knew much.

What did you find out through Link-Up?

The information came back first about my grandmother. Her name was Gertrude King. She was born in about 1900, which makes her about thirty-three when she died, and that she went to Sydney for an eye operation, and all of a sudden there was a child [Paul's mother] on the scene. And she raised the child three or four years, before she died.

Then in the second letter Link-Up gave me some information about having traced some Kings out at Murrin Bridge, and you went out there, and cross-referenced what you'd found out about Gertrude King, and found it was her sisters and brothers out there. There was about five sisters and three brothers out there. She would have made the sixth sister. I was over the moon, looking up maps, trying to find Murrin Bridge. When you put the icing on the cake and said, 'We'll take you out and show you,' that was terrific. It was the best week I've ever had in my life.

The next stage was when I had to organise holidays as soon as I could so I could get out there. Not knowing what I was going to find out, not knowing if I was even going to enjoy it.

I don't know [what I expected to find]. I wasn't sure

if it was tin sheds, or people running around with loin cloths or what it was. You just can't fathom it out, can you? If you're going 600 kilometres you think you're out the back of never-never, and you never know what you're going to find. And going by the bad reports, the negative reports you see on TV, you get the impression that all Aborigines are drunks. And you get the impression that they're just all layabouts.

Did that worry you?

Didn't worry me. It was family. Mum had a pretty rough life herself with alcohol. I didn't know what really to expect, but I was eager to look at what was there so I could appraise it for myself.

SHERRY ATKINSON

I always knew I was Aboriginal. My grandmother used to sit me on her knee and say, 'You're my little Aboriginal girl.' I've always known it, so I didn't have any problem there, but it didn't mean anything to me until I started getting to thirteen, fourteen I suppose. All through my life I suppose you could say [I was aware], but it got a lot stronger when I started maturing. You begin to wonder where you come from, who your mother and father is, if they're alive, how come you're the unlucky one. A counsellor at school I remember, I was having troubles at home and she said, 'Oh, you're fostered and you're Aboriginal, what are you doing here?' sort of thing. She really opened my eyes a fair bit. Putting me down. My foster parents didn't let me watch TV or anything that had anything Aboriginal, really tried to hide me from my culture. They were racist, and they didn't like anyone who didn't have money or a good job, or weren't in the upper class of society. They thought, or the way I think they thought, was that: 'She's our little Aboriginal girl and she's our daughter and she's going to be brought up our way.'

They were turning me into a white person, they were taking my whole culture and my whole everything from me and making me what they wanted me to be as an adopted child. Because I wasn't their real flesh and blood they were going to make me as if I was. No matter what culture I was. That was their aim.

Oh I got heaps at school. 'Abo', 'black'. It's really hard if you don't come from a black family, 'cause you can't go home and say, 'Mum they called me an Abo.' If you did, she'd say, 'Oh the silly white bastards, don't worry about them.' They would have made me feel proud of what I was. But if I went home and said, 'They called me an Abo today,' my foster parents would either just say nothing or they'd say, 'You have to put up with it.' I used to think I was a real reject. I ended up doing bad at school just because of it. I only had one friend at school and she used to be as white as milk! They used to call us the black and white minstrels. Everyone else hated me.

That was Carlingford, upper-classs area, really racist. No other Aboriginals in sight, not one. All they had was not their own ideas, but their parents, and society and media. What's on the front page of the *Herald* this morning: booze, blacks, all the big bad words.

When I ran away it was the first time my foster parents ever trusted me, 'cause I was fifteen, to stay in the house by myself. They left for four hours. But wondering if I'd run away, actually I'd thought about it heaps and heaps two or three months before, but I didn't have enough guts to do it, there was never the right time. So this was a good time. I wrote a letter saying:

> Thank you for everything you've done, I'm sorry I'm not the perfect daughter that you want me to be but I have to find out who my mother is and my family is and where I come from. Don't come looking for me because it won't change anything.

I took off on my foster brother's bicycle and I couldn't ride the thing. But that didn't matter, nothing mattered, I just wanted to go. I had my bag, and I fell off the bike about twenty times even before I got to Gosford, nearly got run over by cars and trucks. Not Gosford, Hornsby, up Berowra way. All I could think of was, 'I gotta get outa here, I gotta get outa here before nightfall, otherwise the police'll be after me.' I was just cycling and cycling, didn't even know where I was going half the time. I remember seeing this path where the bike could have fitted. It was a big racing bike with handlebars bending over, I must have looked a real character to everyone else. I judged, yeah yeah, but there must have been a rock and it made me swivel. Next thing I saw a tree, the road and the gutter, I just sort of plunged into the gutter and fell over, all these cars and bipping their horns and I was thinking, 'Oh shit.' Even that incident didn't scare me or startle me that much, all I could just keep on thinking was 'go go go, find find find' sort of thing.

I kept going till I got up to Berowra and it started raining like hell. There was no way I could be riding in the rain, it was bad enough when it was dry. So I stayed in this house which was empty. I walked in there and I had this candle in my bag. It was getting dark and it was raining and I put the candle on and tried to think what I was going to do, look out the window every two seconds to see if the police are goin' past. I went over to get some fish and chips and by the time I got back it was all cold and greasy. I think I started to sit there with the chips and burning them with the candle, just playing around. Then I decided, well there's no way I can go back, I'll only get in trouble and busted and grounded for a month. Thought I might as well do what I want to do, and go. Oh have a ball, get drunk, all sorts of things that I had never experienced. I had $27 and I thought I was rich, 'cause that was the most amount of money I'd ever had. Fifty cents was a lot to me.

Well I left the bike there, and that made me feel really guilty because we were never allowed to touch each other's belongings, never shared anything. I left that there, standing out in the rain, hitchhiking standing there sticking my thumb out, and I was thinking, 'This is not me.' These men went past bipping their horns but no one would pick me up, and I thought, 'Oh God the last thing I want is a bunch of fellers to pick me up.' Anyway I saw one of these little green bubble vans, I thought, 'Oh great.' He said, 'You're standing in a real bad spot there'—he could tell that I wasn't an experienced hitchhiker standing in the wrong spot, no wonder no one stopped for me. He was American and the girl he was with was German, and I thought, 'Oh great.' They asked me what happened and I said my parents were separated, my mother was in hospital so I had to go up and visit her and my father wouldn't give me any money to visit her so I was going up there by myself. That was the lie that I used. They took me all the way to Coffs Harbour, it was so good. Fed me and everything. They asked me if I had run away, and I said, 'Oh no.'

They let me off at Coffs Harbour, I stayed with them two nights, didn't want to leave them. Then I was hitch-hiking again, it was late at night or something, only trucks were going past. I was pretty scared, didn't want to stop, just to keep on going, didn't know what to do, so I just sorta kept on going. This truck driver pulled up, picked me up and he took me up to Brisbane and I ended up getting drunk up there. He found out my foster family's address by looking through my bag.

He rang my foster father up and he flew up to Brisbane and met me at the airport and this truck driver took me to the airport. He said to me that he was just looking at some planes. I said, 'Oh, yeah', and I was trying to think whether I'd leave. 'Cause I knew I didn't want to stay there, but I was like in a trance, I couldn't think straight or anything. All my pride had gone and everything. Looking into my mind, the worst thing that could have happened had happened. So we walked into the airport terminal and I saw my foster father and it was just too late. I started crying, I don't know why, I still don't know why, probably 'cause I thought I was failure, I'd failed. He said, 'Never do that to me again.' But he was so good about it, I know he cared a lot more than my foster mother did.

He took me all the way back on the plane to Sydney. I was crying all the time, saying, 'Oh what's the foster mother, no, what's Mum going to say?'. He was going, 'She's been brought up hard so you just gotta cop whatever's gonna come flyin' at you, just do the best you can.' I got there and my foster mother—it makes me laugh—well it does and it doesn't. She was sitting there cryin' her eyes out like hell, so upset, but I just thought, 'It's your fault, you made me run away, it's not my fault that I'm Aboriginal and I have to find my parents.' I suppose in a way it's not her fault, but I felt like it was her fault, 'cause she's the one that adopted me. All they could say was 'Where've you been, what've you been doing? You're bad, you're a typical black.'

That made me feel a lot worse after that. That made me feel a lot worse, and I just said, 'Look, I'm going to get a job and I'm going to move out. I don't belong in this family any more, I'm not your flesh and blood, I don't have to stay here.'

'Oh what about all the things we've done for you? What about the education we put you through?'

'Yeah I appreciate it. You've done your job. You adopted me, that's what you do for adopted [children] but you've gotta let go. You've gotta really let go. I'm letting go.'

So I ended moving out of home, having a good time for a while. I had all my bags packed, and when I went to say goodbye I didn't even get a kiss from them or nothing. Ever since I was little my foster mother said to me, 'When you get married we'll pay for everything, it'll be a lovely wedding.' And when I walked out the door, all she said to me was, 'Don't come back to me when you get married.' It's crazy when I think about it. I think it must have really hurt her. But none of my foster parents or family ever rang me up, I was just really isolated. I was at the stage where I didn't know where I'd come from, where my family was, whether they existed, I didn't have a foster family I could fall back on, and I was drinking a fair bit. I was really lost all my pride, friggin' put myself down so bad.

And when Link-Up started finding out about my family I started thinking I was somebody. Yeah, I am somebody, I'm not the only one.

Did you ever have a fantasy about meeting someday?

I always fantasised. I used to cry myself to sleep. I remember ever since I was little I used to cry myself to sleep every bloody night wondering who, where I come from, picturing my mother, what she'd look like, having her hold me, just being in someone's arms, in her arms, being loved. I used to cry myself to sleep, I used to get so angry, friggin' hit my head against walls, I used to get really mad. As I look back now it's so incredible, what it did to me. It's like I was in a prison, something I had no control over, I couldn't get out 'cause I didn't know how. I fantasised heaps. Especially when you told me about my Mum. Oh, every night I was dreaming, picturing what she would be like. Pretty close to what I pictured, too, fairly big, happy. Black. Black! I used to watch movies of families and I wanted my own family, and pictured how happy I should be. My foster family was all fake. They just moulded you in what they wanted you to be. They don't let you grow or develop, they don't give you any freedom. They take you right away from your culture and expect you to have no feelings for it. You can't do that. You get a little Chinese child [fostered in Australia]. Those kids are going to grow up and want to go home, no matter how bad home is, they'll always want to go back home. 'Cause they know, no matter how perfect everything is, they will go back to their roots.

I was with Taxation, sat for an exam. But never talked to Koories. I'd look, I'd look like crazy, and admire and check them right out, pick them to pieces. But I was always too scared, I thought, 'No, I'm different, I'm not like them 'cause I've been brought up with whites, I'm educated, so I'm different.' Not better than them, but I just thought I'm different. Put them as 'them' too. I didn't know any history so I suppose I just took it off the media, took off what society says about blacks, you know: lazy, do nothing but drink, got no initiative. So I fitted into that sort of thought, and it wasn't till I started going to Tranby [Aboriginal College, Sydney] that I realised the true history. People just look at the surface. They'll talk to an Aboriginal, 'Oh, won't employ him,' and they start stereotyping.

KIM CHAPMAN

How did you come to be adopted?

My mother always wanted a little Koori baby. She was in Sydney and she went to the office down there, and they said a little black girl had been born. I was supposed to go to another couple but they weren't ready for me. So they said, 'Well would you like the baby?'. Mum said yes, so that was all fixed up. A couple of weeks later they had to drive out to the country to get me, and they got there to the hospital. Apparently the sisters there didn't want me to go, and as Mum and Dad were leaving with me, the sisters ran out with a toy and a card for me. I think they had a nickname for me: Minnie.

How much did you know about yourself?

Where I came from, and what my name was. I think Mum told me when I was little, and then when I started to worry about it all, she told me again. She told me some things about my mother that she'd been told, and she dug up some old letters and cards from the hospital. So I knew I was adopted, but I can't remember what they said. It never really worried me till I was fourteen. I knew someone else, my [natural] mother and father was out there, and from then, every birthday I used to cry, used to worry a lot. I just felt angry and very hurt, because they didn't want me. I didn't know anything, I just felt they had me and they didn't want me so they gave me away. But on

Kim Chapman, aged 4 with her parents Des and Hope

Kim and her brother George, 1971

the other hand I felt grateful: Mum and Dad are really good. And they were very understanding, because they'd been through the same thing with George [adoptive brother]. Personally I don't think they handled it as well as with me, so when it came to me they were really good, they understood.

Did you get a job after you left school?

Not for a while. Just sat around, and after a while I got a couple of jobs here and there, nothing really permanent. Then I got a job at the hospital. But I didn't really get on with the head lady. There was another Koori working there and she was very outgoing and everyone liked her. I don't know whether it was because I was only young, but they put a lot of dirt on me. One day I was in the boss's office and he was telling me that he had reports that I'd been rude to white people. He said, 'Well you shouldn't feel that way. I'm Dutch and I don't feel strange towards white people'—really putting me down. I didn't like what he was saying. Eventually he got me really mad so I told him he could stick his job. I said that was it. It probably came from the head lady. She never really liked me. When I was behind the desk a couple of times, people'd walk in and as soon as they saw me they'd go, 'Oh!', look at you, and then walk up. Their whole attitude would change. They'd throw the papers at you, but I was never rude.

When did you start wondering seriously where you came from?

I was fourteen, nearly fifteen. Mum and Dad knew that the family had to be from round where I was born except that they didn't know how to go about it. I think because I wasn't saying to them every day, 'Oh, I want to find out,' they didn't really try to find anything. Not until Mum got in touch with that Adoption thing [Adoption Triangle]. I didn't tell them more because I didn't want to hurt them, and because I saw what they went through with George.

I used to picture a father and a mother, and a whole pile of brothers and sisters. I always pictured a big family. I was in the middle. They lived in a brick house. I pictured my father being black, not white. Then I found out my mother's [Christian] name, I think [from the NSW Department of Youth and Community Services non-identifying information]. It said I had two sisters, and their ages. It talked about the father, his name, how tall he was, where he came from. That's about all.

Was it a shock to find out that father wasn't Aboriginal?

Yes. I didn't like it at all. It didn't seem right. A Yugoslav! Oh gee, no. I won't accept it. It was a big shock actually. I thought it was the same father that we'd all have as well. It makes me angry, very angry. If I met him, I don't think I could be nice to him. I'd be very aggressive and very angry. I don't know anything about it, but I feel he didn't care. He just got her pregnant and left her. I don't want any blood of his in my body.

Was it hard for your parents when you got this information?

No I don't think so, but I don't know what they used to discuss when I wasn't there. They said they knew some day I'd want to find out. During that time I'd had a lot of problems and I think they brought the feelings on. So we got in contact with Link-Up to see what could be done from there. Mum brought the Link-Up booklet home and said, 'I think this might help us.' We read it, and she said, 'Would you like to give it a try?'. I wasn't sure. I said no, I didn't want anything to happen. Then a couple of months later I wanted to find out. It really worried me. So we had a phone call to say Link-Up was coming. Finished work and I came home. I met them and I showed them the information I got. They asked a few questions, if I knew the family name, where I came from, had a talk for a while. Then after they'd left, it made us feel good. This was the first step.

Alicia Adams

I came here [to Bomaderry Children's Home] fourteen months old and my brother was three. Well we came here to this Christian Home, and it was all lady staff. We two grew up happy here, same as the other children. We all got on very well together. We used to get up at about six o'clock, it was dormitory-style then. Mum, [Matron Barker] she was matron then, she died two years ago, she used to come round and tell us all to get up and get dressed and we'd have breakfast at about seven o'clock. After breakfast we'd do our works, little jobs, like sweep the verandah: we used to go up to the bushes and get ti-tree and make it into a broom, and we used to sweep the paths and the verandah so Mum can be pleased with us. We used to call the others [other staff] Aunties, you know. They used to take us for walks up into the bush, they used to take us up there and sing choruses. As you know, this is a Christian Home. We used to go up on the highway,

Children at the United Aborigines Mission Home, Bomaderry; Alicia in the middle, 1944

we used to sing there. People used to stop and come over to us, but as soon as they came we'd stop singing. There's caves over there in the bush, they used to take us over there for walks. We used to get sticks for the heaters to have hot water for our baths.

There was a school at Bomaderry and we used to get on well with the white children, I had so many white friends. But we used to take a packed lunch, and they used to wrap them up in newspaper, you know, the lunches, and we used to open our lunch at dinner time and saw all the writing on the bread. Oh it was really terrible and of course with newspaper it looks awful. It was Mr Jordan, he was the principal, he asked them [the staff at Bomaderry] could they not put their sandwiches in newspaper because it was no good. So we started having it in greaseproof paper, but we used to have one big case and all the lunches were packed in there. Sometimes Mrs Boyd, she was our schoolteacher, she just lived down the road, she'd take us home if we didn't have any lunch, you see, because we couldn't eat the bread with the writing on it, so we used to complain to Mrs Boyd and she used to take us down to her place and give us some lunch. Then [after school] we walked home. We used to walk, with no shoes on you know, just dresses. They never had uniforms. We used to come home barefoot, even in winter. We didn't have shoes to wear and our feet were real cold and we used to cry because our little feet were real cold.

I was [at Bomaderry] right up to twelve years of age and in 1953 I went to Cootamundra Home. I wasn't too happy there because, as my brother said, going out from a Christian Home into a Home that's not Christian, you could see the difference. We wanted to have grace. Matron [of Cootamundra] said, 'We don't have grace here.' And I started crying, because we used to have grace before our meals. Oh lots of other things you know, but I really loved this Home at Bomaderry, and I really cried every night just because I missed home here you know, and I was wondering when I was ever going to get back.

When you left for Cootamundra, did anyone tell you what was happening?

No, nobody told us. We didn't know where we were going, Mum took us up. We were on the old steam train, and I felt real unhappy and sad because I left all my friends here and left all the staff here who I loved. Mum sat next to me talking and I thought, 'I wonder where I'm going?'. I thought I might be going to somebody's place to live, but when we got there we saw the big house. There was a lot of girls there, and my mind was sort of confused because I didn't know where I was was and I didn't know the place I was at. But the Matron, Matron Hiscocks, she was really lovely, because I loved Matron and she just came over and put her arms round me and tried to settle me down and, you know. It was alright, I had no problems at the Home really. We had to start learning to do our own ironing and help in the laundry. Well that was good because it was good discipline, but still my mind was on the [Bomaderry] Home, and I was really frightened of the big girls. Because some of them would really give you looks and you sorta stand there shivering, you know, and shaking. This little girl Sally, she was there and she [staff member, Mrs Healey] said, 'That's your sister there,' and I said, 'No way, she's not!' because she's real dark. I said, 'She's not my sister.'

I never ever knew I had a mother or a father. I just thought Mum [Matron Barker] was my mum you know, my white mum and I thought all the ladies were my real aunties, because they were all white and I really loved them you know, each one of them.

Did you worry that all the girls in Cootamundra were Aborigines, but you, as you thought, were not?

Yes actually I did, and I said to myself, 'These people are different, they're dark', and I thought I was white you see. I said, 'I wonder why they're so dark?'. I was looking at my sister Sally and thought, 'Dear, she's really black', and you know, I was really confused. I looked at my skin, and I thought, 'I look brown like them too', but I said, 'Oh no, I'm white. Mum brought me up and I've mixed with white people all my life till twelve years of age and then I went to the [Cootamundra] Home and saw all these other Koories. I must be like them. The same.' And I was real hurt because I didn't want to be brown, you know, I wanted to be white. And ever since I was little I always thought I was white and I didn't want to leave Mum because I screamed when she left [to return to Bomaderry] and I wanted to go back with her and I was tugging her dress to sort of, I wanted her to take me back with her. But she sat me down there and spoke to me and told me, 'You gotta start growing up now, you're twelve.'

Why did you want to be white so much?

Well I never thought about it that way, I just thought I *was* white, I never even thought about it you know, why the others were . . . ah . . . brown. I don't like the word black, so I call them brown you know. I was very much ashamed. I used to wear long-sleeve jumpers, because I always thought I was white up to twelve and then I went to Coota. I realised I was Aborigine you know. I was ashamed, that's when I started wearing jumpers, long sleeves, because I didn't want anyone to notice my skin. But a lot of children in the [Bomaderry] Home thought they were white because I suppose with all the white workers you thought we are all like them. We didn't take any notice of the colour of our skin, what colour we were, we just thought we were like them. At school nobody ever called us black. We were never taught about Aborigines. I never even knew the word Aborigine. We had a full-blood Aborigine working here a couple of years ago and she said, 'Can you cook a damper?'

'No, what is a damper?'

'Don't you know any Aboriginal culture?'

'No, I never ever heard about it. You were brought up with your own people.'

She got so cross because I didn't know.

When I was little here [Bomaderry], there was this man. I think he was real black you know, jet black, and he used to come and visit and ask for bread and things like that. So Mum gave him some bread, but when I saw him looking at me I was really screaming my head off you know, because I was scared of Aborigines. I was real scared of them. I used to cling, and nearly pull Mum's dress off her because of this Aborigine. He tried to walk over to me, I think he tried to make friends with me, I suppose, but I just ran away screaming. I hid under the bed and that night I had a dream about this man and I was really terrified, because we never knew. Our parents never came to visit the children, not one. There used to be Aborigines walkin' in and out here, but we used to be so frightened of them. Mum said, 'Don't be afraid of them, they are your people.' I said, 'They're not my people, no way, they're not my people.' You just thought they came from overseas or something.

Were you happy at Cootamundra?

A lot of girls were happy there, but it's when you go out in the world you're confused and don't know where to go. When I was fifteen they got me a job out of town and I wasn't very happy. I was real miserable you know. Because they used to say, 'Get this done and get that done, you haven't finished your job, you gotta do this', and they'd sort of pile up jobs on you, and being only fifteen you can't do an adult work, you have to do little jobs. I told them I didn't like it here and they got cross with me. I told them, 'I hate it because you've given me too much work to do. You've given me ironing till nearly about nine o'clock at night and polish all the rooms.' They had a dairy farm and they used to wash these things, cream

Alicia, aged 16 with the Matron at the Bomaderry Home

things, and the washing and I was only fifteen. And I was crying with all this work. So I complained to Matron Hiscocks about it, and left there.

[Then] I went to Moss Vale to this Minister's place, but I wasn't happy there at all. They had a two-storey house and it was worse still. You had to get your jobs done and they'd make you do it. And I used to really cry. Every time I'd go to bed I'd be so tired and exhausted. And when Miss Fleming came, I had a talk to her and she said, 'I'll see what I can do about it.' Then she came and said, 'Would you like to go to Bomaderry?'. And boy, didn't my heart lift up then! I was so excited. When I got down there Auntie Mavis, she came down to meet me with this big smile on her face. Do you think I was able to smile back? No way, because I was too shy. I was so happy when I got back here. I got on well with the girls who were about my age, and I used to go out quite a lot, and started going to Christian Endeavour. I've been really happy ever since. When I was about sixteen I became a Christian, and then at seventeen I went to Bible College.

Joy Williams

My story illustrates how some Koori children were placed not in all-Koori Homes, but in institutions where they were the only Koori child there. I had the sense of being different without knowing who I was or why I was different.

What is your earliest memory?

I remember when people used to come and visit at Bomaderry Home. There was a lady came with her lovely silver belt buckle and it was Auntie Nuggo [Mrs Louisa Ingram] and she always used to wear it with this blue flowery dress and I used to think she was my mother.

[I was at Bomaderry] till I was six. [Then] I went to Lutanda, that's a [Plymouth] Brethren Home. [At that time] it used to be in Wentworth Falls and I can still remember the train trip. I had a new tartan skirt and a red jumper and a blue coat and red patent leather shoes. I remember the steam train and one of the workers from Bomaderry took me to Lutanda. I remember we stopped at Strathfield, because the station master, you know how you get the shrubs along the railway station, he had cut them into animal shapes. I remember an emu and a kangaroo. And I remember getting to Wentworth Falls 'cause I was given bread and milk, hot bread and milk, and it was raining and there was another little girl there and she was going to be the youngest. It's funny because I ended up in all the eighteen years, third eldest, so I went from second youngest to third eldest in forty-two kids. Now I was the only Koori kid there.

Were you ever told why you went there, instead of Cootamundra?

No, I was never told of any decision even as I got older. But obviously there was a decision because a few years ago I wrote to the Home and asked them why I was there and they sent me back a certificate that was made at

Lutanda. I showed it to Mum, who'd signed it, but she told me it didn't have anything written on it when she signed it, and that was '47. It says 'Reason for admission: a fair skinned child to be taken from association with Aborigines'.

"Lutanda" Children's Home
WENTWORTH FALLS, N.S.W.

APPLICATION FOR ADMISSION

4 MAR 1947

A 46/3538
6-MAR 47
SYDNEY

Date of Application ______ Date Admitted ______
Name of Child EILEEN WILLIAMS
Date of Birth 13/9/1942 Place of Birth Crown Street Hospital
Name of Mother Dora Williams If alive yes
Name of Father ______ If alive ______
Name of Guardian ABORIGINES WELFARE BOARD
Address and 'Phone Number BRIDGE ST. SYDNEY
Religion PROTESTANT
Why Admission is sought TO TAKE THE CHILD FROM ASSOCIATION OF ABORIGINES AS SHE IS A FAIR-SKINNED CHILD
~~Is applicant able to contribute towards child's support?~~
~~If so, to what extent?~~

A Doctor's Certificate MUST be obtained before Child is admitted.

Signature of Applicant X Doretta Williams

Joy Williams's Certificate of Application for Admission to the Lutanda Children's Home, Wentworth Falls, New South Wales, 1947

What was it like at Lutanda?

Well I've been told I should be grateful. Very difficult! Very straight, very religious. I think I was converted six million times—was saved. That entailed another piece of cake on Sunday! Had nice clothes, always had plenty of food. There was always a big changeover of staff so there wasn't any use getting attached to anyone. [After the Home moved to Sydney] I went to Hornsby Girls' High, was told I should be grateful for that.

When did you learn that you were Koori?

When I was about eleven. I wondered why I didn't have any visitors. They had visiting days, the first Saturday of every month, and I used to wait at the top of the gate

Joy Williams (right), 1949

for Mum. See, at Christmas I was the only kid left in the Home, and they used to sorta draw lots to see who was going to take me home with them, otherwise somebody'd have to stay at the Home to look after me. Practically drew lots. But I wasn't happy with that, that's when I started running away. I spent the night—nothing happened though—with this fellow at Hornsby. Next thing they hauled me down to the cop shop at Hornsby, and that's where they told me. I was given an internal, and I was still a virgin, much to their surprise. And when I got back to the Home, I got a hiding with a butter-pat, and I had to write 500 times 'God is love'.

The only Koori I'd ever heard of was Albert Namatjira! Look at the cuts on me arms. I started doing that when I was about twelve, 'cause I wanted to find out what colour me blood was. Nobody wanted me there—only to work. I was looking after the girls all the time when I was sixteen. I grew up thinking I was ugly and stupid. I didn't think anyone wanted me. I used to watch those kids being fostered out: nobody wanted me. Angry most of the time. Always attention-seeking, whether it was good or bad. That's why I was converted so many times, they were all over you like a rash.

Then they put me into the Nurses' Home at Parramatta District. The majority of [Lutanda] girls went to business college in Hornsby, I went to the nurses' quarters. The first thing I did was to get a picture of the Everly Brothers and stick it with nail polish on me mirror, 'cause we were never allowed those sort of things [at Lutanda]. They were heathen! And I used to sneak in and put the wireless on, real soft, and hear 'Diana', and then I'd have it on ABC and I'd hear Harold Blair, that was nice too, John McCormack. That's where I got used to Beethoven.

Joy Williams as a teenager (left)

How long were you nursing?

Not long! I remember my roster was such that I started off with two days off, so I went back to Lutanda. All the girls went home on their days off, so I went. And they said, 'No, Joy, you can't come back here, you live at the nurses' quarters now, that's where you have to stay.' I was sixteen, just over. I was put into male surgical, doing dirty pans and trotting round with bottles, a nursing aide more, I think. But I ended up at North Ryde as a patient. I had a little six months in jail, on remand, and I was offered either to go to North Ryde Psychiatric or a conviction, and I was cunning enough to take North Ryde.

What happened at North Ryde?

We were put in pyjamas for seven days, then they worked out our medication. Had to go to groups twice a day, I think, and they just tried different things like Stellazine, Melsaden, Triptanol, Tofranil, Largactil—good old Largactil—Mogadon and barbiturates. See when I started nursing one of the senior nurses gave me some amphetamines to keep me awake. I asked her what it was and she said Methadrine and I liked the feel of that. Then I was getting sleeping tablets at night, Phenobarb or something like that, Carbital. Junky! In groups you're supposed to talk about your innermost feelings, and I know it now as confrontation therapy. If you said you felt good, everybody'd be on to you till you felt absolutely rotten, so you weren't allowed to say how you really felt, because you'd end up feeling exactly the reverse. I got pretty clever at that, pretty cluey, and in the small groups we'd turn it round and just practise it on one of the nurses or something.

Then you were allowed weekend leave, and I used to choof off down to the city, and that's where I met the fellow I married. Had me baby at North Ryde. I took off again, and when I came back they got a male nurse to take me over to St Anthony's [Catholic Home, Croydon] with my daughter and I didn't sign anything then. I'm *told* I signed adoption papers, but I was very heavily sedated at the time. I used to be on 600 mls of Largactil a day, then Stellazine and bloody Melsadon at night. Should've killed an elephant. I took off and didn't go back. Haven't been back since.

In the late 1970s, Joy learned that her mother, whom she had not seen since she was a baby, was living at Bodalla on the far south coast of New South Wales.

Well we all went down to Bodalla, asked at the pub where she was, they told us she was out on the Nerrigunda road and so we went out there and we found a shack that Mum had been living in. No one was there, and we went back to the pub and they told us that Mum was up in Nowra hospital. So we stayed at Bodalla that night and came up next day and saw her in hospital. I remember sorta thinking, 'I hope she wants me.' And then the sister in charge of the ward made us wait a while, while they went and prettied Mum up. Prettied her up, eh. She had a dressing-gown on. No, she walked up the hall. I knew her straight away.

She hit me. And she said, 'Hello Eileen.' (Bomaderry changed my name because there was another Eileen in there.) I said, 'Hello,' and I didn't know what to call her. See I got me birth certificate years ago when I got married so I knew her name, and I didn't know whether to call her 'Dora' or 'Mum'. 'Mum' still sounded funny. Doesn't come easy. Then she whacked me and asked me why I bothered to find her, and I thought Rachel [Joy's daughter] was going to kick her in the ankles. I think if it had been a bigger woman and a younger woman I would have slogged her right back and just walked out. It was only that she looked so sick and I was pregnant with Ben. I started crying and then she gave me a cuddle. Then we just stayed around the area till she was ready to be discharged and I took her down to Bodalla, and then I took her back to Sydney with me. I sort of felt she was taking me home, but there was no way I wanted to live in that tin shed. Couldn't handle that because it just seemed so typical. Mind you, my flat wasn't much better, come to think of it.

I suppose I was thinking if I put Mum in a nice place she'll be OK and she won't want to come back there. So I thought the next best thing was to take her back with me. The fellow she'd been living with had just died too. I suppose I always had in me mind, of being able to live with her and being a family. I had a lot of trouble being a mother to Rachel when she was little because I didn't have anything to compare being a mother with. I was hoping she could teach me.

Mum couldn't wait to go back [to Bodalla]. My God, she was out. I mean, she was only up with me just over two months and then she was gone. I had the coppers looking for her everywhere. She's back down there! On and off all the time. She wanted to get back. I just wouldn't listen, or didn't want to listen. I still find it hard to talk about Mum. Part of me still believes what the Home says that she didn't want me. And yet the majority knows that that isn't true. The big majority of me.

Well by then I was well and truly back into the Koori community, 'cause, living at La Perouse, a lot of people up there had been able to fill in a lot of details about Mum and when I came to Nowra—it's a different community, but they all knew Mum, all knew the family. Except no one mentioned Cowra to me. When I first came here I felt like an outsider—well, I *was* an outsider—and the only credibility I had was being Dora's daughter. See in the Home, I'd always been a number. No matter what job I'd been doing in the past I'd always been a number, a payroll number or something, and now I get another label: 'Dora's daughter'. Never 'Joy'.

How did you first hear of Cowra, where the rest of your family were living?

I met Coral [Edwards] at Wollongong, the Aboriginal Community Centre, and Coral was talking about Link-Up. I was there to do Drug and Alcohol [Counselling] because I was working at Jilimi, the Aboriginal Women's

Health Centre, and I'd never heard of Link-Up before. I told her my name was Eileen. She said, 'There are a lot of people looking for you.' Mum had never said anything, even the time she'd been with us. I think Mum was ashamed that I was taken. I think she was hurt and I don't think she's ever gotten over it, I really don't. Then Coral asked me if I'd like to go home. And I said yes. Brave! Like hell. I felt scared, oh it was awful. I had great romantic notions too, oh great romances and fantasies. It wasn't an easy decision. Far from it. It was sort of like, unreal, totally unreal. I remember thinking, I wonder if I'll live up to their expectations; what *are* their expectations of me, and what am I going to call them? So I didn't decide to go home overnight either. It wasn't an impulsive or a snap decision 'cause I knew it was something that would change me.

What was holding you back?

I was ashamed of meself. Very angry with Mum because she'd never told me. Auntie Emma had never told me. But there was still something there. Even the name sounded right: Cowra. But then you said 'mission', and gawd, that bloody done it. All my image of me as 'I'm from a mission.' That's all I needed. Gawd!

I remember when I was in the Home and I was taken out on a Sunday School picnic to Lapa [La Perouse] and all the young boys were diving into the ocean for money and that. And I said, 'How could they do such a thing? I'm glad I'm not one of them, oh dear.' Jesus Christ! Of course, and I mean, we do things much better! Well, we wouldn't even consider doing things like that! I mean, with my past with the coppers and all the rest of it, I wasn't any better than anybody else. And yet I thought I was.

Paul Behrendt

I was born in Lithgow. The family was together there but my mother died shortly after the birth of my younger brother. There were nine children in the family. The family was then split up. My youngest brother went to some orphanage for young babies. There were two older brothers, an older sister and myself who all ended up in Burnside Homes. It was 1942, during the war and my Dad couldn't support the nine children. He had no money and he had no backing from his own family. I understand from limited information that he was ostracised for marrying my [Aboriginal] mother in the first place. Then, when my mother died, he flatly refused to discuss anything about her with me. He seemed to have ruled a line across the book as if to say that chapter of his life had finished. He had done his penance.

Did you see your brothers in Burnside?

Oh yes. We mixed together, but not for very long because the older children left the place. My younger brother joined me when he was old enough, leaving the three of us younger brothers there.

What was it like?

When I first went there during the war, there would have been a few hundred kids there. Quite a lot at any rate. Each house had around thirty children in it, and there were about nineteen or twenty homes. It was a church-run organisation; the children were not committed [by court order as state wards]. It was a 'pay-as-you-go' sort of thing, but my father would not have been able to pay for it. He must have been subsidised by someone. He just lived in a boarding house. In those days the rules were that you didn't go out except that you were allowed to go out once a month with your parents on a day trip. We had no homes to go to.

Did you know you were Aboriginal before you went to Burnside?

Although I always suspected it deep down, the first real confirmation came after I left Burnside. I would have been about twelve or thirteen years old and my father had remarried and I had gone to live with him and my stepmother. One of my older brothers came to the house with a form to join the army. One of the questions was about nationality and he asked my father whether our mother had any 'coloured' blood in her. I think that was the term he used. My father hit the roof and said, 'As far as I am concerned, your mother was white!'. And that's where the discussion ended. And that was the philosophy that he adopted. He just wouldn't discuss the matter any further. Indeed, my stepmother kept badgering him because she obviously wanted him to confess, as it were, but he would never come out with it.

I can remember going to a man who was a mutual friend to them both and who had known my mother in Lithgow. But he didn't want to get involved in the argument and wouldn't say anything straight out, but I can remember him saying, 'She [my stepmother] wants to know these things but I'm not going to tell her. Anyway, they say that with Aboriginal people that it breeds out.' So there was the first confirmation, now that I think back. He didn't say yes and he didn't say no, and that was indicative in itself.

Well I've always known that there was something there without being able to define it. In the forties and fifties there was the instilled attitude that Aboriginal people were hopeless cases. This is why, at school, whenever anything came up in class about Aborigines (such as when they attacked the explorers) everybody used to cast accusing glances at me and I would shrink down in my seat. The teachers used to also speak to me in mock pidgin-English when they had to chastise me. There was always some subconscious thing there. With the barrier that my father had put up, it was hard to establish what it was.

I left my father and my stepmother when I was fifteen

and I went out into the world, and I went through life with this thing in the background. But something happened whenever I entered the same room as another Aboriginal person. There was always this eye-contact without a word being said. It didn't have to be. It was as though our auras mixed. It still happens today but I understand its meaning now. I think that it has always been there; it has just been waiting for something to happen to release it. It was only after I had my heart problem that I realised that I had this thing inside me that needed to be released. It was then that I decided to follow this advice—well, it was more a spiritual directive than advice—to go and find my people, to find out who they were, where they were, and that's how I started out.

RICK MCLEOD

I dedicate my story to my brother Robert (Big Bob). He never lost sight of his goal, and that was to see his family reunited.

Can you remember much about when you were very small?

I remember some things. From what I've been told Mum came to Sydney, and she went to welfare for help. And the only help she got was that they took us kids off her. She was from interstate. There were six: Robert, myself, there was Ronnie that I never saw or knew of, then there was Rachel, Pauline [Schmidt] who I also didn't know of, and Michael.

I was sent to the Royleston Depot in Glebe and then was sent to two foster homes before the Lowry [fictitious name] family took me. We used to have people come in to the Children's Home. They'd look you over, check you out and say, 'Might have you for a day out', or something, but I don't particularly remember the Lowrys. All I remember was that a guy from Beaurepaire picked me

> Roderick was seen on the 29th November 1962 when the Binet Intelligence Test (form L) was administered. He obtained an I.Q. - 89 (M.A. 6.5)(CA 7.3).
>
> Like his brother Robert whom he closely resembles, Roderick is prone to stammer under stress. He responded well although he has a grave disposition.
>
> Although of aboriginal stock, Roderick is not ethnically distinctive and should not be difficult to place. His intelligence level is dull normal.
>
> **Psychologist**
>
> **Report 4.1.63**

An extract from the Senior Psychologist's report on Rick McLeod when he was 8 years of age, 1963 (Department of Child Welfare and Social Welfare)

up one day in a ute, he was a tyre rep. I said, 'Where are we going?'. He said, 'I'm picking you up for the Lowrys. I'm dropping you off at the Lowrys' place which is in Marrickville.' So I'm going there, getting all the good stuff [clothes etc.] and we just went from there. Doing what you're told.

So you were always aware that you didn't belong to them?

Yes I knew that, but they weren't the sort of people you could sit down and have a chat with. We were in Marrickville for a couple of years. Then the foster father bought a farm down the coast and we were there till I joined up [joined the army].

Were there any Aborigines in school with you?

Not that I can remember. Not that I would've taken any notice, 'cause I didn't know I was Aboriginal myself till I was in High School. But I can remember the foster father used to be a bit of a racist. I remember there used to be a lot on TV about the Aboriginals living in missions and stuff, and they'd just show the shanties, and he'd say, 'Look at these people, they don't get off their arses and help themselves.' Things like that. That probably reflected on me all those years, and then all of a sudden finding out.

How did you find out, then?

It just came straight out of the blue. We were working on the farm, I was walking up to the farmhouse and I just happened to look down the gully and [there was] this bloke, he was very dark. Shortly after the foster father came up and queried me, 'Did you happen to see the guy on the back of the tractor?'

'Yes I did.'

'Well'—he was about to make an excuse or something, then he said, 'He was your uncle. He wanted to meet you.'

'Oh yes'—'cause you couldn't say much to him.

'. . . And I thought it in your best interests that he shouldn't meet you.'

That was the end of it. The dark guy went away. Then other things fell into place. But it was never ever said that I was Aboriginal. He never mentioned the subject again. And it was shortly after that that he asked me to go to a couple of private schools. And I said no. Apparently my relations went to the Bomaderry High School, the one I was at. And they were all family down there, and yet I went to school there and didn't know them, or know of them, because my name was Lowry. All the references and reports that I received from the High School were all in the name of Lowry.

Were you ever adopted?

No, but at school it was always Ricky Lowry. The foster parents showed me how to write it down, and that was my name from the minute I walked in their door until I was sixteen and nine months and I joined the army.

How did you find out your real name then?

I didn't find that out till I was at Bomaderry High School when the welfare started giving me cheques for going to High School. A welfare person came round to Bomaderry High School and I was dragged off to Head Office and she said, 'Oh, g'day Roderick.'

'No, my name is Rick.'

'No, your name's Roderick John McLeod.'

'No it's not, it's Ricky Lowry.'

'No, no, you've been fostered, your real name is Roderick John McLeod.'

> According to the foster parent, this lad is progressing in a most satisfactory manner. They state that he is behaving himself well, although his standards of personal hygiene frequently leave a lot to be desired. The foster parents, however, are persevering with training in this regard and are not particularly concerned with this matter at this stage. Roderick is a friendly, rather good-looking type of boy and has settled in the foster home very well.
>
> An application for Commonwealth Aboriginal Secondary Grant Scheme has now been completed and is attached. Previously, the foster father was not in favour of any such payments, as these, to him would underline the fact that Roderick is an Aborigine. This matter has been persevered with and the foster parents suitably counselled and they have agreed to proceed with the application. Application for Education Grant in Aid has been sent to Aboriginal Welfare Dept.
>
> ---
>
> RECOMMENDATIONS
> 1. Note visit
> 2. Note application for Aboriginal Secondary Grant Scheme.

An extract from Rick's 'Periodical Report on Ward', 1970 (Department of Child Welfare and Social Welfare)

And I was really happy when I found out my real name, and that's when all the trouble started with the foster family.

Why was it kept such a big secret?

I surmise that the foster father had four daughters and he wanted a son, possibly to carry on his name. Also he fostered me, being one of the lighter [coloured Aborigines].

So they knew that you were Aboriginal all the time?

Most definitely, yes. But nothing was ever mentioned to me that I can remember.

Can you tell us about the time when you ran away?

I think I was about fifteen [1971], everything was just building up. I don't know why, it just felt uncomfortable. I got really upset all the time. We used to live on the main highway at Berry, and there's this truck broken down at the front, by the main gate. So I sat there watching the truck for a couple of hours, and I said, 'Oh bugger it, I'll pack my bags and I'll get away with this truckie.' It broke down about five o'clock, and I said to myself, 'If it's there at 11 o'clock, that's it, I'm going down and ask for a ride.' Eleven o'clock, and it was still there. So I went down and said, 'Oh listen, I've just come up from South Australia (or Melbourne or something) and I'm looking for a ride to Sydney.' I had my clothes in my bag, about five cents to my name. Hitch-hiked up to Sydney, then out west up past Wellington, Dubbo, up north, got a job in Narrabri for two weeks, working on a tractor, ploughing, then I went to Brisbane, went back through the Moonbi Ranges, got a job down there for a week.

I was away a good six weeks. At Narrabri we used to work twelve hour shifts on the tractor, six till six. We were living in this bloody tin shed with bore water which stunk, but I felt independent, it was good. I was on my own, doing my own thing. I got two weeks' work, I think I cleared about $270. I went to Coonabarabran. I remember this place, walked in to get a pair of shoes with me bare feet and come out with new boots on. Beautiful kangaroo hide riding boots, cost me about $20. New jeans, new shirt, new outfit. Looked like a million dollars. But I earned it all myself. I was rapt.

When I returned home, I walked in the front gate, and my foster mother called to my foster father, 'There's someone here looking for you.' She didn't even recognise me. Just after six weeks. 'Cause I didn't write to them, ring or anything. They said, 'Goodo, where've you been, have a cuppa tea, have a chat, what are you going to do?'. I said, 'It's all right, I'll go back to school, get things sorted out.' So I went back to school, everything was right for a while, then it built up again.

A year and four days later, my foster father bought me a motorbike. I was going to go and do a mechanics apprenticeship. The bike was to ride just from point A to point B, I couldn't ride it anywhere else although I used to ride it round the farm all the time. Things all blew up again. I don't know what happened, I got all frustrated. Anyway, I left on the motorbike this time, didn't have a licence. I was going to drive up to see my friends up at Moonbi again, and the bike blew up outside of Tamworth. I tried to palm it off on this garage guy, and he wouldn't have anything of it, because I didn't have any registration papers. Didn't know anything about that. I just left it in the bloody garage and said, 'Listen I'll just go and ring my old man up and get some money to fix it.' Then I just bolted. But the guy got on to the coppers and they traced the registration back down to my foster father, sent it down to him by train.

Eventually I found my way to Berry again, where all my friends were. I used to live in the hay shed which is next to the house. Had a couple of dollars on me then, and I used to go surfing every day, one hamburger a day, that was all I was eating. Then a good friend of mine, Georgie, he knew my foster father really well, saw me down the main street one day. I bolted but he chased me round the corner.

'Oh, Rick, I want to have a chat with you.'

'Oh yeah, what do you want?'

'When are you going to come home?'

'Why should I?'

'Oh well, you know, the Lowrys miss you, they want to know how you're getting on.'

'Oh yeah.'

'Well come down have a cuppa coffee with me, have a chat and see how things go.'

'All right.'

He was a hell of a nice guy. He rang the foster father who was at golf. Georgie told him that I was with him, and when the foster father arrived he just walked in as if nothing had happened and said, 'Oh, how're you going? How long you gonna be back this time?' Shithead! Went back home. Then my foster father said, 'What are you going to do now?'. I replied that I intended to join the army. He said, 'That's good, at least you won't be able to go walkabout every couple of months.' And that really stung. It took all those years for him to say that. I'll never forgive him for saying that. It hurt. I just shut up. Eventually I did all my tests and passed, and I had to wait three months before I was enlisted.

How long were you in the army?

Six years. In the infantry. There's a lotta corps you can go into, after you do your basic training at Kapooka, but the infantry sounded more exciting than the rest. Turned out a real bummer. [But] there was plenty of excitement. It was a good life.

Did anyone call you names?

Yes: 'Oh, you black bastard', 'you Abo'. To me it was rather a shock. The more they threw at you, the more you don't want to be Aboriginal. You'd say you're a wog or say you're a bloody spic or something, just to get away from your Aboriginality. That was really when 'oh, you black bastard' and 'you Abo' really hit home. They just threw it straight at you. I'd never been called that before. Never. Not once. I didn't get it in Sydney, or in Wagga, but it must have been when I got up to Queensland and got a bit of a tan, and when I start tanning I go black. I thought, these guys are just having a dig, and getting called that all the time I sort of rebelled against it. I used to get really upset, get into fights and everything over it. Calmed down now. It was the invariable argument with somebody. Or on exercises, you used to have to run up hills, and if you weren't running fast enough it was, 'Come on you black bastard, get your arse into gear.' Everyone copped that, but I must have felt a little bit—what's the word—pinpointed, singled out. 'This is in your blood, you should be able to run for miles', all this crap.

How did you feel about yourself as an Aborigine at the time you came out of the army?

Not great at all. I still had a great grudge against my real parents. I went through life believing I was the eldest boy in the family, and me being the eldest, I could accept being fostered out. This is my line of thinking, see, this is my logic when I was in the army. Then I found out I had extra brothers and sisters. I found out they were fostered as well. I thought my parents must be a bunch of bastards if they had other sons and daughters and fostered them out as well. I couldn't accept that. I said to myself, if I ever saw my real parents, I'd knock 'em on their backs for doing something cruel like that: having kids and then fostering them out.

It was the wrong line I took, wrong tack, because I didn't know till four months ago what actually did happen. I felt like a mongrel dog ever since. I remember getting a letter in the army from my brother Robert, and from Rachel. She was in a Home, and when I wrote back, they said she doesn't live here. So that was the end of the contact with her. That was in 1972 or '73. And when Robert wrote, I wrote a letter back to that address, and I never received a letter back. I used to think, seeing they didn't reply to my letters, they didn't want to know me. Mum said the same thing: she used to write us letters. They knew I was in the army, they wrote letters, but they wouldn't be forwarded on to me. They thought, well, he doesn't want to bloody know us, he wants to stay with his foster family. There we are. Both in limbo and here's the welfare or whatever it was bloody getting the letters.

Did you ever deny that you were Aboriginal in the army?

Yeah. Quite often. Quite often. You can accept the name wog. Being called a wog or a spic was a lot easier than being called an abo. There were not many Aboriginal guys in the army either. I even passed as a Maori a couple of times.

What did you do when you left the army?

I worked as a trades assistant for Thomas Borthwicks and Sons. I went under my mate's name so I could get the dole as well, but anyway I ended up getting a permanent job so I had to change my name back. That was quite embarrassing. I spent two years there and the place folded. I've been here now four years at Port of Brisbane. I met Janece about a year before I got out of the army. Janece fell pregnant before I was due to get out. She asked, 'Are you going to stay in?'. There's so many broken marriages in the army, it's terrible. I said, 'No, we'll go our own way, we'll get along.' I've always had labourers' jobs, but we paid the bills.

I didn't know the real story till after our third child Jenny was born. She was crook and in hospital. This little dark girl was there from Mt Isa. Janece mentioned my case to the nurse, [that] I had a big chip on me shoulder from being bloody adopted, and the nurse said, 'Well in a lot of cases it wasn't like that', [i.e., in many cases the children were forcibly taken]. I got real shitty with Janece. I said, 'How dare you talk about bloody me', and all this crap. Anyway, the nurse just told Janece that sometimes they just took the kids for their own well-being. It all came to light. I just definitely had the wrong idea. Maybe I didn't want to accept the fact that I was taken.

So that set you on a whole new train of thought?

Well it did. 'Cause that's when I saw Beverly [Johnson, Co-ordinator of Link-Up, Queensland] and approached Link-Up. I was in a pub. A guy found me in a pub, a Murri [Aborigine]. That was unbelievable, that was. I had two jobs and I was sitting there, after my main job. Having a beer on my own. And this guy comes round and singles me out.

'Who are you.'

'Rick McLeod.'

'Where's your family?'

'They're at home.'

'No, where's your real family?'

'What do you mean by that?'

'Your mother and father, your brothers and sisters?'

'I wouldn't know.'

'Oh, I can put you on to a lady who might be able to help you find your family.'

He mentioned the name Beverley Johnson, so I got in contact with her. And she came round for an interview, and from there it's just history. I'd ring her up every couple of months, and then one day I was looking at the *Courier Mail* and it had a photo of a woman meeting her daughter for the first time. They were helped by the Relinquishing Mothers and Adoptees Association. It had a phone number there so I rang up and said, 'Listen, my name's Rick McLeod and I want to know if you can help me.'

'Where are you from and where were you born?'

'South Australia.'

'I'll send you out the appropriate South Australian form.'

I used to look at all the Aboriginals walking down the

road, and thinking, 'I wonder if Mum looks like her. I wonder if me sisters look like those women,' trying to visualise.

JEANETTE SINCLAIR

When you were growing up in Perth, did you know that you were Aboriginal?

Yeah, I did only because I had mental images of what my mother was like. I could remember her having fair hair and could remember she had sort of a nice figure. But I can also remember she was dark. I mean that idea of her being Aboriginal may have faded a bit, but when I went to live with my father's mother she was never short to remind me that my mother was Aboriginal. She never did it in front of anybody, it was only between her and I when she was being vindictive. It was extremely negative stuff she used to say about her actually, she used to call her 'that black slut'.

Did you fight with her about that, or were you too young?

Well we moved before I got old enough I suppose. I was twelve and my father remarried and then decided that he wanted to take us on as a family again. He'd left it a bit late I'm afraid, but we moved up to Queensland then. He was totally unaware of what was going on because he only visited a few days a year, for the whole time we were with my grandmother, which was from about five to twelve years of age. So he was unaware of what was going on. And because I didn't know him, he was a stranger to me, it wasn't as if I could tell him what was going on in the house either. So when we went to live with him it was like moving in with a stranger. But he was still at sea when we moved in with him. We moved into his house but he wasn't there, he was at sea still. We actually moved in with his wife, our stepmother.

Jeanette Sinclair (right), aged 8, with her sister Bronwyn and brother Gordon.

She is white. That's when I got really resentful about the fact that I had been moved. I'd been moved into another situation where I had no say. I moved out when I was fourteen or fifteen. I only lasted a couple of years up there. I couldn't stand it. I didn't know my stepmother. I moved into a house with a stranger.

And because you are pretty fair, I guess no one at school spotted you as a Koori?

No, nobody did actually. It was really funny when I was growing up. As a kid I used to live out in the sun. I still do, love the beach, love the water, and to get away from my grandmother and grandfather when I was a kid, I used to nick off to the pool all the time. Every day, rain, hail or snow. And I used to get really dark, and my nickname at school used to be 'boong'. But nobody knew that I was Aboriginal. That was just a joke. But it used to *really* hurt me.

Jesus, it upsets me when I talk about stuff like this. Sorry . . . I don't think about these things too often, see. Stupid.

Did you have a friend you could talk to?

Oh no. I remember when I moved to Queensland, there was one Aboriginal at the school there, and it was a really funny situation. I mean, you can look at it with hindsight now. I used to sit and look at her and watch her all the time, she must have thought I was weird. But I never went up to speak to her because I was too scared. And I thought, well what can I say to her anyhow? She may have known that I was Aboriginal, I don't know. It was strange. But there was nobody, actually, that I could talk to when I was a kid. I have a brother and a sister, but they were young.

Did you think being Aboriginal was shameful all this time, or was there part of you that was proud to be Koori?

I thought . . . I was ashamed at the fact that I couldn't say that I was Aboriginal. Not that it was something to be ashamed of, but I was ashamed of myself for not saying I was Aboriginal. Do you understand what I mean? But I felt I couldn't say I was, because people would think I was an idiot, because I didn't look like an Aboriginal. And I really thought the only real Aboriginal there was—because I had been through the school system—was someone that was dark. But I knew that there was some part of me that was [Aboriginal] because I just didn't think and feel the same way as other people round me did. Does that make sense?

Did you know your mother's name at the time, or anything about her?

No, I had no idea. My grandmother and my father wouldn't give me my bloody birth certificate and I didn't know how to go about getting one so I had no idea. I didn't know how to find out things, at least, not those sort of things. I only found out my mother's name through the ex-wife of my father's brother. She came from the west too. She came over to visit Nanna and they wouldn't let me in the house near her. It was because she knew. She went down to leave, down to the station, and as she was leaving she passed me and told me that she would meet me down the shops in a half hour. So I waited for the half hour to pass, and then I told Nanna I was going down the shop, and off I went. I met her down there and we had a little chat and she told me a bit about my mother.

But she wouldn't give me all the information. All she'd tell me was that she knew my mother, that my mother had just given birth to a little girl, which was a real shock to me. What else? She didn't say whether she was married or anything. I was too scared to ask questions, and I just wanted to hear, and her to tell me. But I got the feeling that it was, like, to get back at my grandmother, that's why she was telling me this much. Because they hated each other, those two. She said basically just that she was fine, that she knew her, that she was alive, that she was in Western Australia, that she had just left Sydney a few weeks beforehand. That really got me. Just information like that. She *did* say her last name though, Collard, and her first name's Doreen. That was the biggest lead I'd ever had. So it made all the difference.

And at that stage, what was important was to meet her. I suppose, like all the Link-Up people say, they sort of walk round with these gaps that they have inside them. Well I was walking round like that. I had a feeling that if I met her, the part of the jigsaw puzzle that was missing would fall into place. It was like an all-consuming thing, from the time I moved up to Queensland really, when I was twelve, that's when it became the most important thing in my whole life. My life generated around trying to find my mother. I went from an A student to a student that only put their name on the exam paper. I failed everything up there, never even bothered to try, because I couldn't think of anything else but getting home. But it didn't do any good because there was nowhere to go to find any information. None of the family would talk, they were this silent brick wall. So what's somebody to do when they are in this situation? They became self-destructive I suppose. That's what I did.

[Several years later, after many unhappy experiences, Jeanette ran away from her father's home.]

And then I got institutionalised because I got caught. They found out that I was under eighteen and wasn't living under parental care. So first they put me before the court and told me to go home. I couldn't face going back to my father's house again, so I said, 'Look put me in the Home, I'm not going back,' and that's what happened. Well I ended up in the Home. But not for long though. I hopped over the fence. I didn't like the brand of Christianity they sold so I pissed off . . .

You think you've cried it all out, don't you . . .

Then I came down here to Sydney, hitchhiked down here and got involved with an older guy and fell pregnant. I pushed him and myself into a commitment that in other circumstances I would have run from. Because if I'd gone back up there it would've been five years of institution. I couldn't stand it. I have never been able to stand enclosure.

And then I had Sharmane and she became my life. So everything else became second matter. Finding Mum, even though it was important to me, Sharmane had given me something else to think of. So it wasn't all-consuming any longer. But that only lasted a couple of years and then I wanted to find her again. But having Sharmane was very important. I'd never belonged to anybody or had anyone to belong to, anybody that loved me with no questions asked. Children do that, and if I hadn't had Sharmane, God knows what would've have happened to me.

How long did your marriage last?

Six months. I couldn't have expected it to last any longer for the reasons I married him. For crying out loud, I was lucky it lasted that long. Him and I are the best of mates now.

So you were living by yourself with a small baby?

Yes. That was fun, real fun. I thought I was going round the twist and going looney, I can tell you. Because I'd never really been a child, I didn't know how to relate to a child. Jesus that was hard. I was an old woman by the time I was five. I didn't think so at the time, but when I think back, how I thought when I was five years of age. But we coped, her and I. The biggest regret I ever had, I think, when I think about it is when I can put my daughter close to me and she leans across my chest. I never had that feeling when I was a baby, being close to anyone. That's the thing I was looking for when I was from twelve onwards.

When was the first time you told anyone you were Aboriginal?

There was an Aboriginal girl in the Home, she was twenty-two. Her and I got talking. I was sort of naturally attracted to her, I suppose it was part of wanting to find out more about myself. I remember once when everybody disappeared and we were sitting there playing with each other's hair, I mentioned to her that my mother was Aboriginal but that I didn't know anything about her. And she never made any comments, she never said anything. It was like a secret.

When my sister was sixteen I told her she was Aboriginal and she said to me, 'What proof have you got that we are Aboriginal?'. And I said, 'I just know, I remember.' I didn't say anything about the fact that my grandmother used to remind me all the time, but I said I could remember. And then I managed to get hold of a photograph out of my father, the only picture he had of me as a child and it had my mother in the background, and I managed to show her that.

And then I said something when I was out at Randwick [Technical College]. It came up in conversation. I was there specifically at the Tech because I'd become so frustrated with my life, how it stood. We were talking about how we existed at College, how we paid our way. They were saying, 'I am on TEAS' [Government Tertiary Education Assistance Scheme].

'My parents support me.'

And I said, 'I'm on Aboriginal Study Grants.'

They said basically, 'What are you on Study Grants for? You're not Aboriginal!'

And I thought, 'To fuck I'm not!'. That's the first time I really felt, 'To fuck I'm not.'

'I am so an Aboriginal person. How fuckin' dare you!' And one of the students was telling me what an Aboriginal person was, and I got up and said, 'Well if I am not a blackfeller and you are the judge, what are you judging it on? Have you ever mixed with Aboriginals?'

I mean, I had a hide, I hadn't mixed with any other Aboriginals, but I wasn't telling them that, I [would have] had to tell them everything that had come before that, and it wasn't their fucking business. Anyhow if I tried to explain, I couldn't keep my head together, I'd start bawling in class like I do now. So I said, 'Have you mixed with anybody?'

'No.'

No bastard there had! And they're telling me I'm not Aboriginal—but they don't know any Aboriginals. But they knew, so they say, 'We just know.' But it wasn't good enough. I left Randwick before the course finished because things were hard for me. Not school wise, I was getting some of the top marks there, but I couldn't handle the situation where the students seemed to feel uncomfortable around me after that discussion in the General Studies course. I felt as though they were asking me to—what's the word for it—explain myself all the time. One: I didn't feel like I should have to do it anyhow, but two: I didn't have the answers. I just knew I was [Aboriginal], it was like going on gut feelings. I just knew I was and that was all there was to it. I left there because I got pissed off with the students. The teachers were good, very supportive, but you still had to survive among the students. There were no Aboriginal students out there at all so I ended up leaving.

I left, but I got the study grant through that time, through the guy I had originally seen at the TAFE. I was thinking that I had to have some sort of identification, to say I was one-tenth, one-eighteenth, one-sixteenth Aboriginal, and I thought they would ask me for proof of who my mother was and I thought I'm up shit creek if they ask me that because I didn't even know who she was. And I went in and they understood. And I didn't have to show any proof. I just went in and said I was Aboriginal and I got the impression the reason why, that is, is because so many before me had come in there with the same problem.

Is that sort of understanding common?

No, often it's not good enough just to say it, and that's shit. It's no good. I've often been asked to show proof that I'm Aboriginal and I refused to. Why should I have to? To have somebody say on a piece of paper that I am Aboriginal!! To know who the fuck I am. I do now and I did then. How do I explain it? I knew who I was, but I didn't have the missing pieces, that's why I went along with it. It's an insult, I think, to ask someone to fill out one of these papers. I won't do it. With Tranby [Aboriginal College, Glebe] it made a lot of difference. Gee that place made a lot of difference.

In what way did being a student at Tranby help?

Incredible confidence. It was like it wasn't only classroom education. I learned more out of that classroom than I did in the classroom, and I still got the top marks at Tranby that year. But all my teaching was done outside the classroom in terms of how one relates to another [Aboriginal] person, the different ways of doing things, the different senses of humour. It was just like a whole new world. Even though I knew my mother was Aboriginal,

I was still affected by what I had been taught at school and by the images that came across in the newspapers etc. But I remember always thinking there's gotta be a reason for it. But I could never imagine what the reason was, because I thought it was just me, that I was a one-off case which had happened to be me, I was different, I was strange. I thought all Aboriginal people had their families, I really did. Because I remember a couple of times running into Aboriginal families and they seemed to be so friggin' big and so many of them and they seemed to be so friggin' happy, you know? They didn't have the best clothes but Jesus Christ they looked happy and I thought, 'Well, they must all have their families.' And to me it seemed more important than all the money, to have each other. I didn't understand about all the separation and everything. It wasn't till I went to Tranby that I understood all that.

It was a great feeling finding that out. Great in terms of that it helped me, but it also made me fucking angry. I was very angry that whole year that I was there, everything that I learned just made me angrier and angrier. That it should happen to people, that it should have been allowed to happen, that it was planned to happen to people. Oh boy, that made me angry. Good things came out of Tranby too. A lot of friendships, lasting friendships, and I think that is a problem with a lot of Link-Up people, they don't have long-established friendships with people of other than Link-Up people because they were not given the chance to make deep relationships. Whereas Tranby gave me the opportunity to make long-lasting relationships with people that know who they are in terms of they can follow their family all back and they have always been with the families, always been with their community. I've made a lot of lifetime friends through Tranby and it has made a lot of difference. It gives me more stability.

Nancy De Vries

My earliest memory is with a family at Merrylands and their name was Adderton. And it was at Christmas, and I remember waking up in a grey cot and there was a doll at the end of the bed and it had brown eyes. I must have been pretty small. They were my foster parents, I didn't realise it at the time, I thought they were my mother and father and my sister and my uncles and aunts. It didn't occur to me at that early stage that I was any different to them. But I didn't know I was Koori. It was never discussed. And they had another boy, his name was Ross, and I honestly thought he was my brother. That was it, he was white.

I'd been taken away from my mother when I was eighteen months old. She had tried to keep me, and because of the years, 1930s, it was a shame to have a child out of wedlock. There was not very much employment because it was just after the depression and things were still pretty tough in those days. There were no pensions, it was a very tough time and my poor mother could not find a position to take me with her. And they took me away from her. And they threw her out in the street. Because we were at Corelli [state-run mothers' and infants' Home]. I have seen it written [on my file]. They'd taken me away—and the letter that was there said, 'Why is this girl still living in this hostel? She must leave immediately.' So they just literally threw her out.

I was with the Addertons till I was five. I started school, but I think I must have been a bit of a rebel at that early age because my first day at school I decided I didn't like school and was goin' home. So I was rebelling even then, at five. They were gentle people, Seventh Day Adventist people actually. Very very gentle people and I was given a good home and treated very very well. But the biggest shock in my life came when they got me to get in the car, which was an old T-Model Ford with the running board and all, and I was sitting in the car and I happened to look in the back seat and saw all my dolls sitting up. I asked them why were all my dolls in the back seat, and with that Mr Adderton jumped in the front seat and the old aunt was there, and they had these hankies and they were waving them to me, 'Goodbye Nancy, goodbye,' and I started to cry because I couldn't understand why they were saying goodbye to me. Couldn't understand it at all. Many years later I found out that they had me removed because Mrs Adderton had stated that I was sexually precocious. Possibly I'd seen that Ross was a boy and I was a girl and I was curious!

And they took me to a family in Marrickville that was so different to this roomy home, everything nice, calm family atmosphere, into this family where they were always drinking. The lady had bright red hair which terrified me, and I slept on an old black ottoman underneath the stairs. I went to Chapel St school for about ten weeks I think, and I don't have very many good memories of that place. I then went on to living with a lady who lived on her own with this Alsatian dog, that was at Arncliffe. I remember going to school and being picked on by one child there. She was a pretty little thing with blonde hair, Shirley Temple ringlets, and every time she came round to me she'd give me a broken pencil so I'd get into trouble. Even at this stage I was not aware that I was a Koori. It never crossed my mind.

Until Mrs Williams after about six weeks decided that I wasn't what she was looking for to lavish all her love on. Must have told the child welfare that she didn't want me, and she must have been instructed to take me to Bidura [state-run children's Home].

Bidura is another story altogether. The matron was an obese brute. She had glasses which enlarged her eyes, and she was a terrifying woman. It was there that I found out. I was in trouble again. I think the King died and I didn't stand up when they played the national anthem. They were telling everyone to stand up, and I thought, why should I, I'm eating my lunch. I was promptly put into the corner for this crime, and I happened to turn around and there was this girl who was very dark-skinned and curly hair like an Afro hairdo. I got a hell of a fright and screamed and screamed. I cried, I screamed, I screamed. This nurse came running up, shook the hell out of me and she said, 'What are you crying for you stupid little thing, don't you know you're the same as her?'. I suddenly found out I was a Koori! I was about six, 1938. If a child can be shocked, I was shocked at this revelation that I was the same as this girl. It just hadn't dawned on me.

In Bidura someone came to interview the matron and to pick out a child. By the way, they called it Bidura Depot. You had to walk up this verandah towards the matron sitting there with her glasses, terrifying you in case you made the wrong move. You had to stand there with the usual hands behind the back, head down. You were introduced, you had to shake hands with the lady and say, 'How do you do, I'm very pleased to meet you.' Then they'd discuss you in front of you, then you'd go back down and be full of suspense whether you were going to leave this dreadful place and be taken away by these wonderful people who were going to give you a home and look after you, or whether you were going to be lining up for tea again that night. When Mrs Monsarrat from Chatswood came and decided they'd have me, I went up there and had a reasonably happy life. I went to Willoughby school, and I can remember being a real rebel, raiding persimmon and peach trees. The things I can remember most clearly was that I loved the garden because it was very old and had old sheds, a wonderful place for kids. Pigs trotter soup on Saturday because I hated it.

Until one day I was sent to buy eggs from the shop and I had a school bag on my back. In those days they used to put half a dozen eggs in a paper bag and twist it round. I was running home with them and this friend of the family stopped me and he ended up raping me. The whole time that this was happening he was telling me that this was what would happen when you were married. I remember when he ran away I jumped up and ran screaming screaming home. What frightened me most was where the eggs had broken in the bag on my back and were running down the back of my dress and onto my legs and I didn't know what it was. I didn't know what it was, it was just the most terrifying thing because I could feel it, this gunk running down my legs and I didn't know what it was. I ran into the house and the kitchen was that dreadful bright cream and green that they used to have in those days. She went over, they didn't put their arms round me and comfort me, they didn't even do anything. They just went over to a drawer, got a knife out and came back to me and said, 'If you tell anybody I will cut your tongue out.' It wasn't long after that, that I was back at Bidura. There's no way I can prove it happened after all those years but it did. I was seven. I was made to feel dirty. Really horrible.

I just hated going back to Bidura. Every time you went back there from when you were tiny, you were made to put on one of the nighties. Oh, I hate thinking about it. And this dreadful old doctor used to do an internal examination on every child while the matron was standing there. They made me feel like a criminal when they examined me after what had happened to me at this place. They just made me feel so terrible.

So I was there for a while and in the meantime I was getting to know Aboriginal girls, we were getting to know each other. When we came back we'd automatically seek each other out—Gloria and Violet were two of my best friends. It was funny, the Koori kids were the ones who just laughed and got through it. Our weird sense of humour kept us going I guess. But I was beginning to feel different. I noticed that I was being treated in a different way to other children. I noticed that I was being excluded from things. It was quite obvious, and I was getting a feeling that I wasn't as good as the other kids. I can remember feeling very angry, and that this was beginning to show up in my behaviour, because boy, I was a rebel. I just refused to comply, I was always in trouble. And of course every time I was in trouble I was being told that it was because I was Aboriginal, bad, lazy. The usual stereotyping was very obvious in those days because I think they firmly believed all those things.

Then I think it was the Stephensons at Bankstown. I was in third class, I was eight. It was near exam time. They were quite all right, I shared a bedroom with their daughter, I was sent to school, I had nice clothes and I was being taught tennis and things like that. Until one night I woke up and I could hear the family, mummy and daddy and the daughter Leslie, who was twelve, talking. There was a lot of crying. What's up, what's up? Something's wrong. Later that evening, Mrs Stephenson came rushing in and proceeded to give me a damn good hiding and telling me that I had taught their daughter to lie and that she didn't lie before I came into their house. She'd apparently lied about her results from the exam at school, and rather than face up to the fact that their own child was a bloody liar, they came in and there's the poor young Koori in there who was the best one to blame for the whole thing. So I got a bloody good hiding for that, and the next thing I'm going back to Bidura again.

So Mrs Webster [fictitious name] came into my life. She lived at Strathfield and she had a green dress with white daisies on, it was a *crepe-de-chine* dress. I can remember her very clearly, very clearly. This little brown straw hat on, and these brown suede shoes on. I can remember the day that she took me back to Strathfield. I remember us getting off the bus, and Margaret her daughter came running down the road and she was yelling out, 'Whoopee, whoopee, here comes my new sister.' We got up to the house, and there was Mervyn, their baby. I fell in love with that child from that minute. Here was this little boy who didn't give a damn whether I was Aboriginal or not, who grew up loving me as a sister. When he was about ten or eleven he was being told that I wasn't his real sister, and he was saying, 'Well I'll marry her when I grow up and then she will be part of this family.' Mervyn and I have never had an argument. I love him dearly and whenever I go there he and his wife and his kids all accept me as just Nancy whether I'm a Koori or not.

Mrs Webster was a Christian, and in those days to be a Christian meant that you were very very narrow minded. She was very very uncompromising in everything, she was not flexible at all. She led me merry hell. I can remember the cat weeing in the bathroom and me being woken up in the middle of the night and belted with a piece of wood because I had wee'ed on the bathroom floor. When she caught the cat doing the same thing a few days later she just laughed and told me. Didn't apologise. I remember once that I'd eaten my lunch and didn't eat my crusts. So I wrapped them up and left them in my case. It was during the war and at Strathfield Park that night there was a searchlight display put on by the army, all the people going up to see it. To make it more enjoyable for me, she spread castor oil on these crusts and made me sit there and eat them. The whole time this was going on she was pinching either my arm or my ear. I hated this lady sometimes. I hated her so much. And yet at other times she could be so gentle with me. Being a soft sort of person even as a child, I would respond to this love and I would think, 'She loves me, she really loves me and things are going to be different from now on.' And then she'd turn round and do something to me that was just as horrible as that. These mental cruelties—besides physical cruelties, she was forever beating me—but this mental cruelty . . . She drove me to the point that when I was a ten-year-old child I drank a bottle of stuff in the cupboard that had 'Poison' on it, because I wanted to die. All it did was taste bloody awful, and nothing happened! A ten-year-old child wanting to die!

It was about this time that I began to run away in the night. Looking for my mother. I'd see a car and being a true Koori I'd shinny up a tree. The police being bloody fools would only look round, not up. I learned that very early as a child in my escapades. I took myself off into the Births, Deaths and Marriages [Registry] one time, trying to find out who I was and where I came from, and that man told me my mother's name. While he was telling me my mother's name they were ringing the police telling them I was there. I just hated. I was very very unhappy. I used to cry at night, not loudly because I probably would have got a hiding for it. There was a need in me to know who I was. I knew I was Aboriginal. I would see Aboriginal people and Mrs Webster would say, 'Look at them, look at them, aren't they dirty, aren't they awful.' They didn't look too bad to me, and they'd be looking at me, they knew that I didn't belong to this woman. She'd take me down to Yarra Bay beach [La Perouse] and say, 'Look at them, all dirty, all drunk.' They weren't drunk! She was forever trying to tell me how terrible Aboriginal people were, how bad they were, how dirty they were, how drunk they were. But I didn't believe this, I wanted to run up to them and say, 'Do you know Ruby, my mother?' I couldn't of course.

In between, with many many years of living with her, being sent away, being taken back, being sent away, being taken back—in between all this I was put on Mulgoa Mission with the Aboriginal children there [Northern Territory children sent from Alice Springs in 1942]. In my white way of thinking, I had threepence ha'penny in my pocket, and this boy called Jock carried my bags for me up to the women's dormitory, and I took this threepence out to give him because this was the done thing in white society. They all laughed and said, 'No, we don't do that here, people do things for you because they want to.' I remember feeling very very embarrased by that. I loved it at Mulgoa.

I was moved again, and this time the Church Missionary Society had control over my movements, so they put me with a Reverend and his family. I was in High School, about eleven. He tried to interfere with me sexually, up in his study. He was pretty near to doing it, his filthy hands on me. I remember running away and I told a lady up the road who was one of the parishioners who thought he was a saint. I was immediately branded as a liar, a cheat, typical Aboriginal behaviour, and removed from them. It was there too that it was brought home a bit more about being a Koori, because I was given an Aboriginal name because they had a daughter called Nancy. I always remember thinking, well why couldn't they change her name? I was nothing, I think, but a cheap babysitter, because I seemed to do that full time when I wasn't at school. In those days children were liars: nowadays if a child says this, thank God it's investigated thoroughly, but in those days it wasn't, and because I was an Aboriginal child I think it was probably hidden even more. And as I grew up I never ever had a boyfriend, to go to the pictures, dancing and all that sort of thing. I think that the things that were happening in my life were frightening me. It was probably making me think that sex was a vile dirty filthy thing.

Then, I think it was just after this man had sexually interfered with me, I was at High School, and they took me away from there, not telling me anything, and they put me into the Reception House. It might have been just after he had interfered with me, and because I'd said it, they were trying to say I was mad. I remember I was there for three weeks, being assessed I suppose—but my God the food was wonderful. You just sat around in bed all day, I mean, I loved it. And of course being so young the nurses just thoroughly spoiled me. It was like a big holiday. It was a new thing for me to be spoiled! But they decided that I wasn't crazy so I was sent back out to Websters. So I didn't stay there long. Forget where they sent me after that. I think they sent me back to Bidura, then back to the Websters. I know I was in Dalmar Children's Home. Didn't last there long, because one of the kids who called me a black bitch, got tied to one of those long irrigation hoses. I dragged her down there by the hair, tied her up and ran the hose up and down on her. Went away and left her. So I wasn't there for long. Back to Bidura, back to the Websters. I've found letters written by Mrs Webster stating that because of my Aboriginality I was not capable of living up to her standards. She set [she wrote] very high standards for her and her children and I was not capable of living up to them, and maybe I would be happier with the dark people. So I think this was about the time the Aboriginal Welfare Board decided that they'd better take me over. They sent me down to Cootamundra. I was uncontrollable and they thought that this would be the place that would really straighten me out. Needless to say, it didn't.

I can remember running away from there and drinking bore water because it was so bloody hot out on the road and thinking, 'God I've poisoned myself,' and I was that glad when the police came along in their car and caught me and took me back. I was very very sick when I was there and nobody believed me till I collapsed one day. As I was getting better there was a big bottle of aspirin, and how lucky I am to be here today, because I took half that bottle. I reckon that the spirits were not going to let me go easily. I think they had a purpose for me later. As I look back, I think everything happened to me for a purpose.

After they took me away from Cootamundra they thought they'd send me further into the bush to be with my people. So they sent me to Moonahcullah [Aboriginal Reserve] at Deniliquin. I loved it there. Loved it. It was a free beautiful life. There was a river, there was swimming, there was a beautiful big orchard across the river to raid, great big Murray cod at breakfast time, great big dust storms that turned day into night, there was kicking around fungus footballs at night that had been soaked in kerosene for about three or four weeks. These are the memories of these places. There was old Dinny who'd take us into the bush and make us listen to the sounds and show us tracks. He was a fullblood, a delightful old gentleman. There were trips into town on the back of the truck. There were delightful beautiful times sitting round the fire at night being told all these stories that frightened the hell out of you so that in the end you'd have your back to the fire and you'd be looking out—you didn't know what was sneaking up on you at night. Old hessian huts with dirt floors that were immaculate. Cooking those Murray cod in the morning in the old camp oven. It's just something that I will never ever forget.

But I didn't last long there. As Koories well know, you

fight. Koories fight, but Koories love. Koories fight but Koories get over it the next day, but of course the whites couldn't see that. The whites only saw me as a troublemaker. They sent me away, though I think they had the hide to say that I'd said that the children were silly. I couldn't believe that, because that was a very very happy time for me there. I don't remember ever saying that. I certainly didn't put them down as people because they, well they weren't *my* people, but they were Aboriginal people, the same as I was Aboriginal. There was a bond there.

When I came back from Moonahcullah I had stone bruises on my feet so I couldn't wear shoes, and I had an old grey overcoat on so it must have been winter. And lo and behold, we walk into the old [Aborigines Welfare Board] building down there in Bridge Street with the marble floors, and there's Madam Webster waiting to greet me and forgive me and take me home again! Okay, it was nice, it was nice to go home again and have a hot bath, have my feet looked after. One of the nicest things about going home was getting between two clean sheets. I had missed that but didn't realise it till I came back to it. But of course our relationship fell to pieces again, I kept on running away looking for my mother, so I was put into the Girls' Shelter. Which I'd been threatened with all my life, that if I didn't behave myself I'd be put into it. Finally the day comes and I'm put into the Girls' Shelter. I'm terrified. Right, this is it. When I got there I had a bloody good time, it wasn't too bad after all. Went to court, I think she [Mrs Webster] came, she spoke for me, she took me home and started again. I just was not going to settle down and accept what these people were trying to make me do. And accept their attitude towards me as an Aboriginal.

Finally I was charged, one final last time, with being uncontrollable and I was sent to Parramatta [Girls' Reformatory]. I think it was nearly four years later, after being held prisoner at Parramatta and going through some pretty horrific things in that place. Being punched to the ground by this man, being locked in a cell for twenty-four, forty-eight hours as punishment. It was tough. The kids today don't know what tough is, they don't know what survival is. How on earth I did it I don't know. I used to read a lot, I had a very imaginative mind and could dream off into my world, I could imagine I was with my family, I'd met my mother, I could make myself cry at the drop of a hat when I thought about how I'd greet my mother.

It was while I was in Parramatta that I got my first ever photo of my mother. It was taken in the evening when she was only young. She had a light-coloured frock on, the old two-tone shoes, only a little black and white photo. And she was sitting down on the grass and she was holding me at the Addertons. Years later when I spoke to Mrs Adderton about it, [she said] it was near the time my mother thought she was going to be able to get me back, that she had a job at Ivanhoe and she was sure she'd be able to get me back. But they wouldn't let me go with her. Mrs Adderton told me that she came out to see me one last time. She cried and cried and cried and she had to go away and leave me. She was apparently told that I would be better living with white people and it was best to, you know . . . She would never ever be able to have me. I kept in touch with them because I think she was a link. If my Ruby wants to get in touch with me, she'll know that I'm here. But they moved from Merrylands to Carlingford so I don't know if my Ruby ever went back there to find me or not. Or to try to ever see me, or catch a glimpse, you know? The Addertons sent it to me in Parramatta.

[At Parramatta] I hated them. There is no other word. A child is very sensitive to feelings, to attitudes towards them. I may have been a little bit more sensitive than others, but I *knew* that they despised me. I found in my papers, 'We feel that this family [Websters] have regretted taking a member of such a despised race into their home.' I couldn't believe that shit when I read that. You know, I hadn't been wrong as a child. I was lucky getting my papers 'cause it helped me come to terms with what I'd done as a child.

When I read all this bullshit that's in my papers, I thought, 'That's why I did it. They don't know why I was playing up, they haven't got a clue. They didn't take the time to find out.' I hated them, I hated the whites. I hated them. And we [all the Koori girls] knew they hated us. They called us these dreadful names—gin, lubra. One girl did have fairly thick lips, and the superintendent used to call her 'Lubra Lips' and the girls'd all laugh. Didn't matter how that girl felt.

I think it's important that people realise that these kids that were taken away from their families, separated from their culture, their identity, had to put up with dreadful, dreadful things. How many of us have survived sane I don't know, and I realise why so many of us have died through alcohol. I was lucky, as I grew up, that alcohol never agreed with me. Instead of the slow death of alcohol I tried the quick death of pills or hanging. I always tell people I cut my wrists here cutting a jam tin, because it's very embarrassing admitting that I tried to commit suicide. I tried to kill myself. I was lonely, I was unhappy, I wanted my mother, I wanted my identity, I felt cheated, I wanted to be me. And I wasn't being me.

I was sent away to the Reception House again. I had such a wonderful time I came back and told all the kids—we laugh when we think about it. It is written down in my papers about how there was a mass attempt at suicide. We plotted it that we would fake suicide attempts! It was a prison. There's no other word for it. A child's prison. Where you did bloody hard labour.

But I managed to escape from there a few times. By this time escaping was becoming an adventure. Just running to get away from them: they weren't going to make me a maid. They sent me to a few places to try to get me to be a maid. To me it was a nice ride into the country, gettin' out in the bush. Then back to Parramatta. Back to the Shelter. It was just one vicious round. My name's carved in there. I hope they keep it as a museum to the government's cruelty to children.

I was finally certified as insane. But it was a ball. I

was about fourteen, and being the youngest patient there really paid off. Because you were spoiled. Then I was sent up to Bloomfield [Mental Hospital, Orange]. I met a wonderful doctor there called Dr David Morgan who knew bloody well that I was not insane. I realise now what I was searching for, but I didn't know then. I found security in having my day ordered for me. It was an easy life. I wasn't expected to work, you can do a job now and then, but if you didn't feel like working you could just play up and they'd say, 'Oh she's having an off day', so you wouldn't have to work, you'd get away with it. And you got three good meals a day, good clean bed to sleep in, you had a hot shower every day, good feed, entertainment, pictures, dances, picnics, I mean, you had everything. Why should you give that up?

All this time I knew I did not want to be a maid to white people. I had other ideas. Maybe a bit high for my station in life according to the white society, but I wanted to be a nurse. I met a male nurse out there and I fell madly in love with this man. This man was sixteen years older than me, he was married. But he would have been the most gentle, considerate man I have ever known. He was so patient with me. He knew how I felt about having sex. He never pushed me, he was gentle, he was caring, he made me see that sex wasn't a frightening thing. I went with him for four years, then finally we got a flat together, and finally I fell pregnant with my Peter, my first son. And my Peter is a child that was born from love, born from pure sweet love.

So I started life with my son, the first living person that belonged to me, that I could say he was mine and I was his. I think that this is why now Peter and I have such a lovely thing going. He was the first thing in my life that could look at me and say I love you and I could hug and love this child and know that I couldn't be sent away or rejected. After twenty-three years of being rejected in your life, this is pretty special.

Well I just went on through life, I battled for many years with Peter, I married a man when Peter was little which was the biggest mistake of my bloody life. I became a nurse's aide and made a marriage of need, not love. He was a very violent man and I left him when my daughter was born because he started to be very cruel to the kids, he was punching the hell out of me all the time, he was not working, he was sitting at home when I went to work with all these kids, he nearly drove me mad. He nearly drove me mad. I finally packed up and left him, and I worked very very hard bringing up my kids. In the meantime I found out I had cancer, it had spread a fair bit, and I was terribly worried that this was it, I was going to die from cancer. But I had a very good doctor, and after many months of being so very ill, I finally survived that. I have survived it because that was eight or nine years ago now. I worked hard, and got them all through school.

Then big changes came into my life. I was accepted into college to do my Diploma of Applied Science. Two years ago when I was doing this, finally I made contact with a Ruby ——. I was moving into my house, and I suddenly realised [at the Housing Commission office] that I'd been talking to a Koori whose name was —— [the same name]. I rang up, I rang his boss. He rang Dubbo airport and got the man to ring me. He answered me on the phone. I said to him, 'I only want to know—do you know a Ruby ——?' He said, 'Yes that's my aunt, she lives at ——.'

which was the biggest mistake of my whole life. I became a marriageable age and made a marriage, of need, not love. He was a very violent man, and I left him when my daughters were born because he started to be very cruel to the kids, he was punching the hell out of me all the time. He was not working—he was staying at home when I went to work with all these kids. He nearly drove me mad. He nearly drove me mad. I finally packed up and left him and I went out on my own. [illegible] bringing up my kids in the [illegible] through. I had cancer once and spread a tiny bit, and I was terribly worried that this was it, I was going to die from cancer. But I had very good doctors, and after many months of being so very ill I finally survived that. I have survived it because that was about [illegible] years ago and [illegible] worked hard, and I got them all through school.

Then big changes came into my life. I was accepted into college to do my Diploma of Applied Science. Five years ago, when I was doing this, finally I made contact with a Baby ——. I was moving into my house, and I suddenly realised that the Housing Commission officer I had been talking to, a Koori whose name was —— (the same name). I rang up. I rang his boss, [illegible] the man to ring me. He answered me on the phone. I said to him, "I only want to know—do you know a Baby ——?" He said, "Yes, that's my aunt, she lives in ——."

TWO

Homecomings

Jean Carter

Jean Carter had returned from Maroopna to Sydney. Sally, her eldest sister, came to visit her. Jean had not yet visited La Perouse, where she had grown up, partly because by doing so she felt that she would somehow 'let the [Cootamundra] Home down'.

So you were making contact with your family by now?

Yeah, Sal was the first. Chicka, Sago, then Andy, they used to travel with the boxing. I always had a good idea of Andy, he used to write and that. He could have been anything he wanted to be, he was that brainy. Anyhow he just got in with this boxing thing, just moved around, never settled down. 'Cause all the family was all broke up [by the Welfare Board].

What about La Perouse?

I'd been back once. I went straight to the Ella's place. I remember, this was when I came up from Maroopna, staying in Crown Street for that two weeks, before I had James. One of those days I came out to La Perouse. The house wasn't there, but Mrs Ella was. She made a cuppa tea. We'd been real close, if I wasn't there, they'd be over home. They asked was I going to stay and things like that. I don't know why I went out, I didn't think any of the family'd be there. We were all in different places. Tommy, he was up in Kangaroo Valley, Sal and I had heard that he was up there. But he found it hard to come to us. He'd never ever stay at Wreck Bay long, just a day or a night, then he'd come back into Bomaderry.

When was the last time you saw Ruth?

When I left Cootamundra, she would have been fourteen. *[Link-Up eventually found Ruth, at Jean's request, in a South Australian town, where she was the matron of the local hospital.*

The two sisters met for the first time in twenty-seven years in March 1985.]

Did it feel strange living among Koories when you first came back to Wreck Bay?

I used to feel different for a while, but it was good, because they were a real friendly mob. People always used to come to the house. And the language was a bit different, you know. There was a couple who used to always come down, because there was a different sheila in town I guess, check you out. And they used to sit up and yarn all night, that was something I liked. Tell me stories. Like this boy, he used to say, 'And the lad did this' and 'The lad did that', and I wouldn't ask, and I'd say to Sally after, 'How come Alan Ladd was in all this? Do they only have Alan Ladd movies down here?'. And she burst out laughing. She said, 'What do you mean?'. Well, 'The lad did this and . . .' And she started teaching me: 'No, "the lad", that means, "that person".' Not Alan Ladd the movie star.

And I knew Sal was a bit embarrassed about giving me damper, just little things like that. I knew I was being treated as if I was a white person in that way, and they used to say I talked different from them. But I fitted in really well there. 'Cause Sal was married for over ten years, she never had any children, so James was the centre of attention. When he started toddling, Sal's husband made him a cot out of all the driftwood that was around, and he used to have this little bed in the kitchen because that was the warmest room in the house. They seemed to be always watching him. I didn't wanta sleep in the same room of the house with him and they used to growl at me, 'Oh you gotta sleep in the same room.' Couldn't afford to have another room anyhow! And they said, 'Don't let that baby cry.' Such and such a thing would happen—there'd be all these ideas around if you let a baby cry. I was more or less told off. I used to be horrified when they'd go to pick him up all the time. 'Don't go picking him up!', but in the end I'd just give up. 'Oh no, he's gotta be picked up when he cries.' I think that's what helped if there was any sort of strangeness there, it would be those sort of things. Good feeling, you know. And I wasn't made to feel ashamed in that community, or in that home. [Outside the Koori community] I used to feel that, when you're not married and you have a baby, that was terrible, in those days, but you just grew up with kids there. It was good to see him fitting in. But that was one of the things that made me feel I'd let them down [at Cootamundra], you know, Mrs English and Matron Hiscocks. I was always on guard if I saw anyone come into the place that wasn't Aboriginal, and I didn't know whether the welfare [would come].

It wasn't really till I started reading Link-Up material that I started to understand what had happened. But I never told my kids I was in the Homes. I was ashamed. It wasn't till I went to Link-Up and got reading that I was able to talk about it. 'Cause I guess [to me] it was something my mother and father did, and I wasn't going to talk about it. I wasn't going to say I was in a Home because me mother and father couldn't look after me, although when I was growing up I used to blame them. All sorts of mixed

Jean Carter

emotions. But I never doubted that they didn't love me. I knew that.

Did you ever talk to the adults at Wreck Bay about it?

No. I think Sally would have had to do a lot of explaining about where I'd been. And there were other families too—every year there would be children taken. They used to walk over the rocks. They never went to school, there'd be no kids in Wreck Bay when they knew the welfare was coming. But it was hard to put it into place, what was happening. Now everything is sorta fitting together, you can see what was happening.

I wonder if you were a bit more different from the others than you realised?

Yeah. I used to always be particular how I looked. I used to put the iron up to the fire, and I was thinking, 'Oh, this contraption.' When I first started ironing I'd get black all over the clothes because you put the iron up to the fire. Sally'd be saying, 'You gotta rub the iron, clean the iron before you . . .' Oh my poor sister.

The first time at Wreck Bay I remember was sitting all in the one room, big fire going, and yarns being told, ghost stories and that. And I was thinking, 'Oh, dear, these people are superstitious, there's no such things as ghosts.' Anyhow, I found out there was such a thing as a ghost. This night I went, I said to Sal—we were talking up at Auntie Ella's, we used to go from house to house, that's what the community used to be. We were up about a quarter to eleven at night, and I came down, and said to Sal, 'James is asleep, I'll go over and get him now, it'll save getting up early in the morning.' And I thought she said, 'All right.' So I started up the road, got to what they call the Sandgut and I saw this thing going along the other side of the road, walking. When I stopped, it stopped, just like the form of somebody. Anyhow I stopped and this thing stopped, walked a couple more steps. Checked out it wasn't shadows or hair hangin' over me eyes, and the second time I started walkin' this thing started walkin'. The third time I just walked straight over to it. I musta been stupid. Walked straight over to it, and as soon as I did I just froze. Just this feeling went straight up me back, and every hair on me head I could feel standing on end. And then it just disappeared. I turned around and I started walking back. I wouldn't run, but I forced meself not to look over me shoulder, and I walked back. And I ran from Beach Road down, nearly knocked the door down. Sally said, 'Where was you?'

'I told you I was going over to me room tonight.' She nearly grabbed me: 'In here you silly bitch, you're mad. I told you never to go up there. Never go past that Gut at night. Told you that . . .'

'Well I just saw something up there.'

When I said that, she dragged me by the hair in that room, 'Get in here . . .'

Even Cyril, me brother-in-law, when I'd said there's no such thing as a ghost said, 'I'll go and show you one.'

Who do you think it was?

Well it wasn't a bad spirit, because Rexie was telling me he went to sleep up there and someone brought him home. But [Sally said] if you'd had went any further something would happen to you. It was warning you to get back.

STAN BOWDEN

When I first left the Homes, the manager at the time, he said to me, that I'd pass as a white man, not to mix with any blacks, and that me mother and father were dead. And then after, when I joined the merchant navy, when I was in Sydney, I used to go drinkin' round Redfern, and that's when I found out that I had other brothers and sisters. I stayed there for ten years in the merchant navy. But things were a big puzzle for me. I couldn't figure out why

I was told that me mother and father were dead and that I [wasn't told] I had other brothers and sisters. Then I got curious and went up to meet the other brothers and sisters. Then I found out that me father was alive. I went over and seen him, but it was two weeks after that that he did die anyway. I never bothered to go back to the merchant navy, I just hung up around Griffith, Condobolin and all that, drinkin'. I think it hurt me in a lot of ways. So I never ever bothered to go back to sea. Because I couldn't figure out why they told me he was dead, when he was still alive.

How did you find out that your family came from Griffith?

I can't remember who told me. I was in the Empress in Sydney, and someone asked me me name. When I told him, he said, 'Have you been up to see your sisters?'. I said, 'What sisters?'. He told me I had sisters up in Griffith, Condobolin. I decided to go and find me family in Griffith.

[I was] confused. Angry too, but I couldn't see at the time whether it was anger or confusion. I think that was where I went drinking a lot. I became an alcoholic. I think because I couldn't talk to anyone about it. I didn't know how to talk to anyone about it. But all the time I was travellin', things were going through my head all the time about the family. I couldn't figure out how everyone else talked about their families, and different ones would ask where I was from. I didn't know. Where I was really from. It bugged me a lot, and I was hitting the grog a lot on the ships. Who I was related to, who I was and all this. Everywhere I went, the first thing Koories would say to me was, 'Where do you come from?'. I never had the bloody faintest. I was never told, and I never had the birth certificate or anything, because to get into the merchant navy, the Aboriginal Protection Board sent all the papers to 'em. Everything was done through the Protection Board, I had no say. I learned a lot from travellin' and mixin' with other people. But even though mixin' with other people a lot, on different ships, different towns and that, I still never knew nothin' of meself. I'd see psychiatrists a couple of times, tried to do away with meself a couple of times, cause I was just confused. 'Cause I'd run into different ones in the pub and they'd say, 'Oh you're related to me in such-and-such a way', and I could never figure it out.

What happened when you went to Griffith for the first time?

I was that frightened goin' up there I got drunk. I had to get drunk, I was so frightened, I didn't know what I was going into. I'd never been on a mission before that. I can't remember clearly what happened because I was that drunk. I was paralytic. 'Cause I was frightened. It was the only way I could've gone back by meself. But I stayed there, going backwards and forwards between Griffith and Condobolin, going backwards and forwards drinkin'.

There was something missing, but I just couldn't . . . I'd met them but I couldn't talk to them about anything. 'Cause they wouldn't talk about anything. I found out that they'd all been through the Homes too. And they wouldn't talk about it. Couldn't or wouldn't, I don't know what it really was. And this was what made me want to find Florence, seeing she was the youngest sister out of the lot—I'm the youngest in the family—I thought that she might be able to tell me about what the others were not talking about. I wanted to find out who, where, why.

I was, in a lot of ways, more confused than ever. 'Cause I still couldn't find out anything about me mother and father. And when when I found me father, I couldn't talk to him, 'cause I didn't know what to talk about. I'd sorta gone over to see him, and planned to go back again and have a talk, but I found out that he died, and I just went back to the funeral. That hurt me a lot, 'cause after leaving Kinchela, when they told me that he was dead—and then finding out that he was alive, all this time I could have gone up and found out a few things, but it was too late then.

How many years do you think you were on the grog?

Ten years on and off I think, going between Griffith and Condo. Then I was gettin' sick of meself, and I started travellin' inland. I ended up in Darwin. I got jobs while I was travellin' through, just enough to keep me going to the next town. All the time I had it in me mind that I'd run into Florence, 'cause I never knew where she was, and I just hoped that if I kept travellin' that I'd run into her. Which never really came anyway. I was drinkin' heavily as well, the drink was gettin' worse.

I was in Darwin for a couple of years, then that cyclone hit and I stayed about six months after, then I hitchhiked from Darwin down to Mt Isa, and I ended up on a pension there. I was two weeks gettin' there, and when I went to put meself on the unemployment thing, they took one look at me and sent me to hospital. The doctors put me straight onto a pension. I never even had a say in that.

From Mt Isa I went to Sydney for a while, just drinkin' around Sydney. I was about thirty-five, thirty-six. I'd met [my other sisters] Lou, Isabel and Bertha, and brothers George and Lenni and there was another one, Sunboy, but he was already dead. I never met him.

But I never stayed long. 'Cause I was still trying to look for Florence. I knew she was around. I'd met her for half an hour after I left the Homes when I was fifteen. That was the first time and the last time. That was in Drummoyne, in Sydney. She was getting married. [After that] everywhere I went I was just asking around. I'd found Lou, Bertha and Isabel asking round in the pub, and I thought I might've found out about Florence through the pubs. I didn't know where to really start, I was just playin' it by ear. And then, I dunno, I think I seen a lot of Koories drinkin' and dyin', sort of made me think that if I kept on drinkin', then I was gonna die too. At this stage I didn't really want to, because I wanted to find Florence. So I went to the Health Commission in Griffith and asked them to send me away somewhere. They sent me to Albury. To get away from the grog. I knew it, I could see meself goin' down quick. The Health Commission tried to put me in a few places, but that was the only one that was vacant, there was a new place in Albury opened up, so they sent me down there. I think I could just see what was happening to a lot of other Koories. That's what made me see the light.

So I arrived in Albury with a garbage bag with a change of clothes. The Health Comission took me down there. The AA thing helped me a lot, because I could talk more, not about the family, but about other things. The counsellor took me to all these places, took me out, introduced me to people. Some good friends down that way. The rehabilitation place I went to closed down, and two of the blokes that was in it, the three of us moved into a flat. One bloke was drinkin', he'd never make it home of a night. The other bloke was goin' down to Melbourne about once a week or so, and then I found out he was drinkin' too. So I went and seen the agent that I was renting the flat off, explained everything to the agent, and asked if he could change the locks. Which he did. I locked the other feller out. When he came home I told him I didn't want to drink again. He went away and I haven't seen him since.

And were you still looking for Florence all this time?

Yeah. After I moved to Albury I got off the grog through the AA counsellor, and I found out that her husband was in the Royal Navy. I went down to Melbourne and I seen a welfare officer—this was the first time I'd talked to any strangers about it, about the split up of the family and being in the Homes and that. A lot of times I used to be frightened of talking about being in the Homes because people'd think I was in a Home where they put bad kids. That's why I never mentioned about Homes. I told this welfare woman that I couldn't read or write properly, and she wrote to the Police Department and Missing Persons and they traced the sister to Dubbo. But they said they couldn't go interstate. So I was back to where I was again, and I didn't know where to find out. So I just stayed in Albury for about eight years. The AA counsellor, he was good to me because he helped me a lot. In mixing me in with other people. See I couldn't talk to people, because everyone else knew where they was from, who their parents and grandparents and brothers and sisters and all this. Everyone asked me this, I still didn't know, so I just kept to meself all the time.

At what stage did you hear about Link-Up?

At different times I talked to a niece, Isabel, 'cause I found she was pretty good to talk to, and she was interested in family 'cause she felt a lot was missing too. She told me she used to talk to her relations, but never got any headway, the same as I couldn't. So we talked a lot about the splitting up of the family. Then one day Isabel moved to Canberra and heard about Link-Up. She rang me and told me. It sounded great to me because I thought all me problems were finished with.

PAULINE MCLEOD

Pauline McLeod, having been raised by a European family, was working in the Department of Youth and Community Services as a trainee District Officer and so was able to call up and read her own file as a state ward. Some time later she heard about Link-Up.

A LIFE TIME

I think I am gonna die
Or maybe just fade away.
My expectation I just
don't fully understand!
I come to meet them,
For the first time in 24 years,
To put aside a life time
of dreams and fantasies.

Is she thin, is she tall
Is she fat, is she small,
Is she kind, is she good?
I wonder if like her I look!
Is she quiet, is she loud?
Is she happy, is she proud?
I will have to give up all my dreams,
And now I must face reality, so it seems.

Throughout my life
I wondered what they were like.
I dreamed my dreams,
I wonder if I was wrong or right.
I come to meet them,
For the first time in 24 years.
To put aside a life time,
Of fantasies and dreams.

Dad is dead! I wonder why?
Why did he go? Why did he die?
Did he want me? Did he care?
Is there common things we share?
How did he take it, when his time came?
Would I like him, be the same?
All these questions that I ask
Will all be answered. Finally; At last!

I remember reading about Link-Up. When I went down to R. there was a circular that went round, we all read it. I remember reading that, and I looked for it, found it in the filing system, yanked it out—it was the only copy we had. And it really got to me. I thought, 'Heck, this is exactly how I feel.' I rang yez and there was an answering machine that answered and I thought, 'Oh dear, I'll give 'em a chance the following week.' I was at the stage of being a total coward and saying, 'If it doesn't answer, if no one answers, I will not follow it through.' They answered. I was real professional, gave out all the information and hoped for the best.

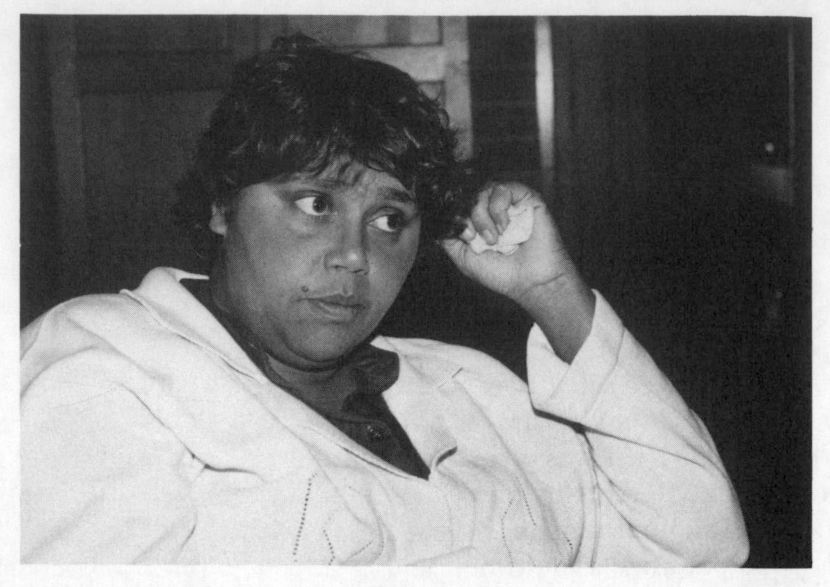

Pauline McLeod at the time of the interview for *The Lost Children*

Then came the real conflict with what I was doing and with what I had been brought up. After all, I was a Schmidt [adopting family's name]. How could I do this to them? And feeling like a real traitor in the process. But not caring. Thinking, 'Oh well this is for me.' So I wasn't able to tell anyone. I didn't trust people in the office, I couldn't tell anyone in the community because word would get back real quick to Muda and Papa what I did. I wasn't ready to tell them and I knew they weren't ready to hear what I was going to tell 'em. So I chanced it and decided that I wouldn't tell them until I met the family—if I was to meet the family.

What do you remember about first meeting Link-Up?

I don't remember. Excitement. Lunchtime. We had lunch in the little cafe. It was really straight to the point, which was great. I needed that as I was as nervous as anything. Not knowing what to expect other than that you had made contact with the natural family. I was really excited because I thought—Great! Finally. You told me the various information about Auntie Eunice, and various members, and you told me about Dad, that he had died. I decided to stay calm, cool and collected and not do anything stupid. I was quite saddened about Dad, but was also excited that the other members were willing to see me and that it had taken such a short period of time. I was really happy that I was going to meet them.

Then we went to see your family in Cabramatta [Sydney suburb] and sent up some photos. What did you think of them?

Just a big wow, kind of thing. This is my family, this is my flesh and blood. These people, on these papers, were members of my family, extended and natural family, and I loved it. There was a picture of Dad. I thought, this is the way he looked. They were strangers, but they were people who had borne me—yet very much they were strangers. So the excitement was there that contact was going to be made, whatever happened would happen. I was preparing myself for anything. I was understanding the facts about Rachel and really felt for her. The meeting [with her] when I was thirteen was coming back to me and I was remembering things. It was an absolute high. I had to tell someone, so I selected one particular person in the office who really understood. It was about the second week before I left R. and he was just very happy for me. He said, 'Good on you', and I thought, 'That's enough for me.' Packed my bags and prepared to leave.

A lot of thoughts were in my mind about Dad. I just seemed to be dwelling on him. He had died before I was able to contact him and I was really feeling hurt. All along being secretive from my foster family and thinking if they ever found out: disownership, total disownership. So Hidden Feeling Time again. Going home, happy, bouncy, pretending everything's all right. All along, all my life, this was the climax, something I'd been waiting all my life to do. Thinking of all the scary things, all the possibilities that could occur, possible rejection, possibility that everything could just fall apart.

[Pauline decided to ring various members of her family before meeting them.]

People in the natural family started ringing up. Here I am talking to Robert [eldest brother] first, he was giving this projection about how everything was great and fabulous, how he was zooming up to see Ricky [McLeod, see pp. 140-44]. I was told that Ricky was found and he wanted to meet also. And a bit of sadness was coming over me, I was realising what I had missed. When Robert rang, Mum was there [with Robert] and she had a very bad cold. She said, 'Oh I love you, daughter', and that kind of stuff, and I thought, 'Yeah, sure', and hanged up. Rachel rang and it was great. That was a real excitement.

Then Mum rang again and this time her voice was different. Her cold was over. I didn't recognise her. She said, 'This is June Lawson', and I thought, 'Who the heck's June Lawson?'. Then it occurred to me and I thought, 'What a stupid thing to think.' Then she said a few things to me, how excited she was, how she's been waiting for this for a long time, how Ricky was going to come down. I was so excited. In the end she said she loved me, she really loved me. And I hanged up the phone, went back to work and then a few days later I felt cranky and upset and angry. I didn't know why. Then I realised: she said she loved me. All these years she never contacted me, and she loved me. How could she? How dare she? I was actually thinking that: how dare she love me? She doesn't even know me from a bar of soap. How dare she love me? How could she love me anyway? Then it sunk in that she really did care. The time was getting closer to the meeting, and I was really going through this 'What am I going to do?' situation.

[After speaking to her brother Robert and her mother June by phone, Pauline met all her family at once in Sydney in August 1986. Rick McLeod had already arrived with his family from Brisbane when Pauline arrived a couple of hours later at June's flat.]

Rachel, Pauline and their mother, June Lawson, on the day they were reunited in 1986

I was trying to be calm. I had no intention of making a fool of myself. I wanted to be good . . .

It was great to see Mum. She was very special. I was scared because I didn't know what would happen. They were so nice, so kind. They accepted me for what I was. It was beautiful. And I really did feel I didn't have to act, I didn't have to fight for love. I was home. It was one of the most relieving feelings I ever had. I felt comfortable with them, I really did, and I knew that none of them would ever attempt to do anything that would hurt me. That they wouldn't make fun of me or think I was stupid or a fool. I was their sister. It was great not having to be a *big* sister. It was great to be where I really belonged. It was so fabulous. And then you gave me that album with the card it was the icing on top of everything and I thought, 'Yeah, I'm home, I'm really home.' It was just an incredible feeling. It wasn't so much calmness, it was just the fact that I was being accepted really, for the first time in my life. I didn't have to pretend any more. I loved it. I felt like it was forever. That short period of time was just forever. It was great. I loved it.

Mum told me on Saturday night about the hard times that everyone had. I thought, 'Heck, what I had to face was nothing compared to what they had to face.' It was all right to let them think that everything was all right for me—what good would it do if I told them what really happened. Just get them upset and angry and hurt them even more than what they'd already faced. But I had to ask Mum about the scars [see p. 21] and what happened, and finding out it wasn't her after all, wasn't Dad after all. That really hurt her and I thought, 'Well I can't tell her any more. She had enough, she knows about Michael [foster brother who had returned several years earlier] she knows about Rachel, she lost a son. What good is it if I told her other things? I just let her think that everything was all right. Maybe one day when she's strong enough to be able to handle it.' But oh dear. It was really one of the most . . . Great. They were beautiful people. They really are. Dad was Aboriginal. It sank in. Mum was Aboriginal. Our whole family was an Aboriginal family. There was nothing that the people in the office could ever say that would change that. I had a heritage now. For the first time in my life I knew where my people were. It was just fabulous. To find my family was one of the greatest things I've ever done.

Paul Cremen

Paul Cremen was living in Nowra when he discovered that his mother, who had been raised in a Catholic Home and had since died, had relations living at Murrin Bridge Aboriginal settlement. These included his mother's aunt, Mamie King, who told Link-Up that she would very much like to meet Paul and his family. He made the journey in August 1985.

As the hours passed—we left here at seven in the morning, I think we met you at ten—the excitement in the kids' faces was growing, because they didn't know what to expect either. For them it didn't matter, they were hauled out of school. They didn't care where they were going, they were going on holidays. But they were excited. It was hard to explain to them that they had family that they didn't know about, because they've always lived close to their mother's family here. They didn't know what it meant to drive six or eight hours and find these people, strangers, that they didn't know. Same as me. I suppose I was the biggest kid of the lot. So as we got there we weren't really tired, which was surprising, because it wasn't just a matter of going somewhere and settling down in a hotel. That was the beginning. We had lunch in Temora, big park there, and got to Lake Cargelligo about 3 p.m. I was feeling pretty good. I wasn't even tired. Usually after a trip to Sydney and back from Nowra, I've had it. So we got out to Murrin Bridge, about twenty to four, I think it was.

When we first got there, the first thing that impresses you is all the houses are similar. There's all kids running about everywhere—I presume they all knew that there was a couple of strange cars coming in the afternoon. We were taking a critical look, I suppose, because when you go somewhere new you always pick out things that stick in your mind. You see a few broken windows or a few screen doors broken in, this sort of thing: 'What sort of a place is this?'

When we found Mamie's place, she came sheepishly out the door, she didn't know what was happening. She came out real shyly. The last time I saw Mum, Mum's hair had gone all white. She looked more Aboriginal as she got older, Mum, her features just seemed more Aboriginal, and when I saw Mamie, the first thing I could think of, was that if Mum had lived another ten years she might have looked like Mamie. I think that was the first thing I said, was that she looked a lot like Mum. And I didn't know how to approach her, whether to run up and give her a hug, or say hello, dig me foot in the sand, or what to do. Just sorta said, 'Hello.' You introduced us, I think. You broke the ice 'cause we were just standing there looking at each other, looking round. She was all right, she was a little bit distant, because she was as shy as us, obviously.

I was impressed with her house, it was a really nice house. She kept it well. We walked through one room out towards the kitchen at the back and there was a little bedsitter room, a little lounge on the right as you walked in, as you walk through the kitchen/dining room. There was a bedroom to the left of the front door. [Another] little old lady lived out the back. That's all I remember. I didn't know what I was doing, it was all a big dream.

[In the kitchen] she had a big sideboard thing, coffee cabinet, with padlocks on it. She used to carry all these keys around. That impressed me, because she said, 'We'll have a cup of tea.' And she got all these keys out and she's fiddling around trying to find out which keys matched which padlock. She locked the teapot away, even, which was strange, but when you got to know her—she looks after things. There was a table right in the middle, and a fireplace off next to the back door. And as you go out the back door there's a sink to your left.

She made cakes and everything, she spent the day making cakes for us. She made a pot of tea—it was as strong as anything. She put two shovelfulls of tea in the teapot, you could stand the spoon up in it. Remember that? We talked. We didn't talk, actually, we didn't know what to talk about. 'Cause she can't run off her life to me, and I didn't know what to say to her. I think I introduced my wife first off and the kids next. So I just grabbed some photos of Mum, hoping it might strike up a conversation. Because Mum was her niece, but by the same token, it was one she'd never seen. I can't remember much about the conversation after that. I think it just trailed on about the kids. The kids helped break things up [otherwise] I don't know what I would have done. We didn't talk, actually, that much. It wasn't till the next day that we actually got conversation going.

[After a short tour of Murrin Bridge, Paul and his family returned to Mamie's house.]

Then we came back and had another cup of tea and went back to the hotel. We asked Mamie what time she'd like us to come out next day, 'cause she wanted us to come out again, and she said, 'Oh, about one.' I thought, 'She hasn't seen us all these years, and we then sorta get on, and she says, "after one".' I thought, 'That's a bit strange.' But she was just as shy as I was, I suppose.

We went out the next day [Tuesday] at one. We went walking round to see everybody. We went over and had a cuppa tea, then she took us to one of her sisters' place, then we went round to Archie's, and found he was 95 years old, he was an older brother. I found out, did a bit of family tree, found out who was alive and who was dead and how many brothers and sisters there were. But things were awfully cold. And it just felt strange. I didn't feel very happy, actually, I felt bored. Anyway, on the Tuesday afternoon, it was pretty ho-hum. We were just walking around, introduced everyone, took some photos, wrote some little odd notes in a little book, who was married to who and who had so many children, all the begats and begats. Then the sun went down, then we all left for tea. I said to Kath [Paul's wife] the next morning, I said 'I don't feel right. It's not working out.' I felt really out of it on the Wednesday morning. Not boring, but it's pretty ordinary after a while. Then we went round [back to Murrin Bridge] at the usual time. You [Link-Up] went to Condobolin at about ten and we just sorta had lunch and ambled up there. I thought, 'We'll give it another day and see how things go, otherwise we might go back tomorrow, on Thursday.'

We went over there to Mamie, as usual, went to make a cup of tea. And her sink was blocked up, funnily enough, and here's me works in the sewerage department, unblocking sinks and sewer lines and stuff. And I did notice when we were walking round the day before, that the Murrin Bridge kids were pulling all these rods they use to clear all the chokages in sewers. So I said to one of the kids, 'Go and get us the rods.' And I unblocked Mamie's sewer for her. Full of tea leaves and stuff. I don't know, it seemed to break down that wall. From then on, the atmosphere was better. She said that no one would've done it for her and she would've had to ring someone up and they would've taken three or four days before they got out there, so it was just as well I was there at the time I was. It broke down the barrier. From then on, everything was really close. It was a lot easier then.

I found an opportunity to do something for her, that she needed doing. Something that didn't worry me, having to put my hand in sewage, I thought it'd be a good idea to get this done for her, 'cause I know what I'm doing. It seemed to help her and it helped me. And Kath in the meantime was with the kids, and they kept Mamie company. Mamie was telling Kath, 'Oh, nobody would bother coming up and doing that for me.' And after I came back, she was really happy. She seemed to have changed. I don't know what she was expecting when she knew I was coming [to Murrin Bridge], I thought it would be more opened up than what it had been up to that point. From then on—blow it. I didn't want to leave. Ever.

[On Thursday] Allison [youngest child] got sick and had to spend the night in hospital. That was the day I invited Mamie into town, she was going to do some shopping. I said, 'We'll have lunch and we'll take you home later.' She came in, Kath went up to the hospital with Allison, and I had lunch with Mamie. We got to know each other. Then, strangely enough, she had one of her cousins in hospital, so we went up to the hospital and she saw Kath and Allison. Then I ran her home, came back on Thursday night when the kids had gone to bed, and I think we [Paul and Link-Up] spent about three hours downstairs talking.

Were you beginning to feel it was worthwhile by now?

It went in different peaks. The excitement of going up and actually meeting them, that was one peak. That sort of broke away. On the Tuesday afternoon it was meeting all the family, which was pretty mundane, when I'd come up to see Mamie, mainly. Wednesday I had to fend for

Paul Cremen and family at Murrin Bridge, 1985

myself and we had the problem, which broke the ice. Thursday was the day Allison was sick. Friday: we went up there for about an hour in the morning, had a cuppa tea. That was sad: the fact that she lives so far away, and you just don't know when you're coming back. Let's face it, if you're going to do it on your annual holidays, it's going to be at least twelve months, and she's so old. You get the impression that maybe you'll never see her again. It was very sad. My wife and I were all teary all the way back to West Wyalong. It was a well worth trip. As I said, it was the highlight of my life. I just can't wait till I go back.

SHERRY ATKINSON

Through Link-Up Sherry Atkinson learned her mother's identity, and that many of her relatives were living at Deniliquin. In January 1985 she set off with a friend to meet her family. The plan was first to meet a family friend who would arrange introductions from there.

Sherry Atkinson

Well all the way down I was picturing my family, what they were like. Started getting pretty emotional, worried, whether they'd accept me, all the feelings you get just before. I went down to Deniliquin and the first relation I met was Pamela Ross, she was a nurse. Drove past, checked the number, looked at the house, drove past again, looked at the house again, drove past. About the fourth time I said, 'Yeah this is it, we've gotta stop.' I started walking over and there's a large lady sitting there on the verandah. Walked up a bit hesitant, 'Oh are you Pam Ross?'

'Yes, yes, are you Sherry?'

'Yes.'

'Oh come in.'

Big hugs and kisses. It was so good just to meet someone. I looked at her, I looked at myself trying to think, 'Do I look like her? Are we the same?', trying to pick characteristics straight away. Maybe she'll be like my Mum.

Stayed there coupla days, then it was New Year's Eve and it was my birthday, and some of the relations from Mildura had come over. My Auntie Lona had come over, all drinking and that sorta thing, but I wasn't drunk. By the time she came over I was pretty drunk though. Everyone's partying and I'm celebrating my birthday and everything. She looked at me and she went out the back and kept looking at me all the time. Wiping, putting her hand on her chin and rubbing. She said to Pam, 'Who's that girl there?'

'Oh she's Christine Farrant's daughter, Sherry Farrant.'

'Oh.'

Thought a bit, then she goes, 'Who's your father?'

'I don't know who my father is.'

Felt a bit [ashamed] saying I didn't know. She thought a bit, 'I know your father.'

Oh my God! Tell me, tell me! I thought, she's drunk, she's just teasing.

'No, your father's Gerald Atkinson.'

She started crying and I started crying and huggin' each other and I'm thinking, 'Oh thank God, I know my father.'

'Oh your father'll be so pleased, he talked about you a lot.' And she was telling me how she tried to get custody of me, my father and all my uncles didn't want to lose me. So good. I wanted to leave and go straight away then, but it was a Saturday and the banks weren't open. I had to sit there and wait for two days. Looked over the map [of how to get to Mildura, where Gerald lived], knowing the map inside out. All I heard about him was that he was a great person, he did heaps for everyone, that he had remarried and had four children. I said, 'Auntie Lona, I don't think I'd better go, I don't want to get into any domestics, maybe he doesn't want me back.' She was going, 'No, he would love to see you. Yvonne [Gerald's second wife] has known about you ever since they met.' She'd even said to Dad just after I got adopted out, that if they can't have children of their own, that they'd get me back. So that was good. But I was still scared because you never know.

We drove down, looked at the house. Wanted to run in there, but I didn't too. Just sorta walked up and got to the front door. Yvonne came. I said—I didn't say Dad,

I don't know why—I just said, 'Is Gerald Atkinson there?'
'No, he's not at the moment.'
Looking at me, she said, 'Are you Sherry?'

She knew! It was like they were already expecting me! Come in and have a cup of tea! Yvonne goes, 'Oh I'll go and get your brothers and sisters.' And I thought, 'What, brothers and sisters? Oh wow.' I was a bit nervous, and I didn't really know what ages they were. They all come in and checked me out, looked at me, went outside and giggled, come back in and have another look, come in again, and in half an hour they're all sitting there looking at me, 'Where the hell did she come from?' that sorta look in their eyes. They're seven, eleven, twelve and fourteen [1986]. Bit of an age gap.

That afternoon, all the news had gone all over Mildura by then, 'Gerald's daughter's back,' and everything, and some of my cousins started coming over slowly. All meeting me and kissing me and I'm trying to get an idea of what my father had looked like. Looking at them, big eyes. They're going, 'Oh he's going to be here soon,' all standing round out the back, and I'm getting really jittery. Then this car comes into the driveway. It was a Ford. Comes in, there's two men in it. I didn't know which one was my father, and I whispered to my cousin, thinking she'd be understanding and wouldn't make a big deal out of it, 'Which one's Dad?'. She burst out, 'Oh she wants to know which one's her father', all laughing at me. They laughed for about a minute and I'm going, 'Well, which one?'. Everyone else is busy laughing and I'm looking trying to work out which one! One was dark and one was really black. I thought, 'He couldn't be, he's too short.'

The other one had a bit lighter skin, and taller. He looked at me. Looked at me, shook his head and looked to the ground, looking at me again, and he just knew straightaway. He started to cry, this was before we even started hugging, he was crying. I was in his arms, 'Oh my baby girl's come back home, my first daughter.' He thought heaps of me. Just holding me and all my cousins, all my brothers and sisters, Yvonne, all crying, it was really unbelievable, everyone was so emotional. For about five minutes everyone was reminiscing. Dad couldn't stop touching me, gripping me so hard on my hands. For that moment I just felt like that little girl again. Felt really protected and 'I'm home.' My Dad, my blood, these are all the nights that I cried and screamed over, it's here, for real, and nothing can hurt me any more. I thought, nobody can do anything to me any more. Dad had never had champagne in his whole life. I had a bottle of champagne in my car but I was just planning to drink it [later] but I brought it in. He looked at it, 'Champagne! I've never tasted it in my life.'

We all sat round the table, and me and Dad were sitting really close—couldn't sit any closer. He was telling me everything. Then all my uncles started walking in. They were just like Dad, crying. 'Cause I was the first girl born, of all the brothers. They all used to play with me. It meant heaps to them, and if they didn't cry right on the spot, they'd take me for a walk and then cry and tell me how they felt. Unbottled everything. Me and Dad, the next day or the day after, we went down the river and he told me the whole story about him and Mum, how things weren't right, how they split up, how Mum had been through the Cootamundra Home, so I think it falls back on that. She was only sixteen when she had me, so she was a victim, one of the stolen generations. So I understood the circumstances. My father told me the whole story and it was so good just to know everything.

Then off to see Mum. Didn't want to leave Dad, had such a ball over there, treated me like an angel, it was so good. So off to Mum. Travelling down to Murray Bridge. I was a bit hesitant, a bit scared I think because I knew that she would feel guilty about the past. But I hoped she didn't, you know? But I went down there, pulled up in front of her place. When I was driving down there I was a lot calmer, 'cause I'd met one half and I knew that things would turn out, it's all right. 'Cause I've got Dad. So when we pulled up, I couldn't find her at first anyway. I ended up going to the hospital. They had a thing on her but they wouldn't tell me her address 'cause it's against policy. So I went to the police station. Just walked in real casual, I said, 'Have you seen Christine Farrant?'. He goes, 'Oh yes, she lives just down the road.' Oh, true!

I pulled up in front of her house and I saw the curtain move. Oh God, she's seen me! But I was a lot stronger this time, I wasn't as scared. I walked up and she walked out. All dark. She looks at me.

'Well, long time no see, eh?' Real casual.

'Been a while.'

'Do you know who it is?'

'Yeah.'

'Who?'

'Sherry.'

'Are you sure?'

'Well I know you're not Rhonda.'

Rhonda? Who's Rhonda? A sister? Sorta clicked on.

She hugged me and kissed me, took me inside, started crying. I stayed with her for a while and went down the river, introducing me to the locals. Mum seemed so happy to see me. I understood her. I was just sorta torn between two feelings for my parents, understanding both sides. I said, 'Look I'm going down to visit Adelaide.' She said, 'Oh drop in to your aunties.' I said okay and took their addresses. But I just couldn't stay there, you know, to think and understand the emotions I was feeling. I just wanted to go you know. I remember her holding on to me really tight and she said, 'Give me something.'

'What, what do you mean, give me something?'

'Give me something to hold on to.'

'What do you want?'

She took my bangle, my necklace, everything I had on me.

'I'll keep these until you come back. Don't go for another eighteen years again and leave me. Come back.'

'Yeah, I'm only going for a coupla days and I'll come straight back, don't worry.'

I drove away. I looked in the side mirror and I could see her standing there crying. But for some reason I just couldn't go back there myself. I just felt confused. I just didn't understand it all. I had to get away and think about it, try and mix things up. I'd got Dad's point of view, and now Mum's, so I had to work things out why.

So I went to Adelaide and thought and thought and thought. I thought everything out. I went back and I said to Mum, 'I want to talk to you in the kitchen.' So we went in the kitchen and I had a good talk to her. I said, 'Look. I didn't tell you that I already met Dad because I just thought that you'd get upset if I had've went and got Dad first rather than seeing you. But it's just that Dad's closer. Just sorta went on the way, I was just going to come and see you first anyway.'

'Oh yeah, that's all right.'

'Well what about Rhonda?'

She looked at me. I said, 'Just tell me the truth. Everything's okay, I love you for whatever. Free yourself. I love you, you don't have to prove anything to me.'

She replied, 'Rhonda is adopted as well.'

I just hugged her, you know, patted her on the back.

'It's all right. I know the things that you went through, you're my Mum.'

She sat down and said, 'I feel a lot better now.' She was so pleased that she got it off her chest too.

But ever since then, I wrote to her and I got a couple of letters from her, and now I haven't heard anything from her. Last year I was thinking of going down trying to find her.

After that I went back to Mildura, but only stayed there for a couple of days because I had to go back to work. But I came back to Sydney content.

KIM CHAPMAN

With the knowledge of Kim's birthplace, birthdate and family name, it was fairly easy to make contact with her family. When Link-Up arrived at the town of her birthplace, however, they learned that Kim's mother had died two years after her birth. Kim's grandmother, it seemed, had not known of Kim's birth and at first found the news of her existence hard to accept. It turned out that Kim's birth had been kept a secret from all except two of her mother's sisters, who had since left town. A certificate provided by the local hospital matron proved that Kim was, in fact, her mother's child. But Kim still did not know of her mother's death.

Because she was only seventeen, living at home and very close to her adoptive mother, Link-Up decided to give Mrs Chapman the news rather than tell Kim directly.

Actually I remember the day that you rang Mum to tell me that Iris had died. Mum didn't tell me, because that day we had to go to a funeral. And I'd left work early to go to my auntie's funeral, and something was very strange with Mum. She was very quiet. And we came home and I was going to go down the road, try to cheer myself up, and Mum said she had something to tell me. She said, some bad news. I said, 'What?'. And when she told me, I sat down and I more or less shut everything out. I went outside. I was more or less walking round like a zombie. I didn't want to hear anything or say anything. I sat in the car, I don't know for how long. Eventually I came inside and felt really strange. I wouldn't talk about it at all either, and it wasn't till a couple of days later, I was going to bed and it came out then. I cried and I cried. I had anger inside. I was punching the pillows round and things like that, I was that angry and hurt.

I think it took about three or four days. I just felt a great big hole inside, I felt so lonely and angry. Because I thought I'd found her and had answers to questions, and then I felt she'd been taken away from me. At first I didn't want to know anything [about the other family members]. Just left it for a while. And then after I got over the hurt and the anger I thought I might as well. Then Link-Up made another visit. They got in touch with my family, and my family did want to see me. I think we made arrangements from there.

[Meeting them was] exciting and scary. Very scary. But also a lot of excitement. Then it was the same as I used

The Chapman family (left to right) George, Hope, Des and Kim, 1988

to do: I started to picture them then. I knew I was going to meet my nanna and sister. Then I got a letter from Vicky [older natural sister]. I had the address of where she lived, and I wrote a letter, and I waited and I waited. Mum was at work this day, and this big fat letter arrived. I opened it up, and these letters fell out. I was jumping up and down, I couldn't believe it. I don't know how many times I read that letter telling me all about the family. I rang up Mum and read the letter out to her on the phone: 'I'll show you the pictures, I'll show you the pictures.' After I talked to her I flew up to the shop and I showed her the pictures and she read the letter. And the lady who had to sign the letter so that Mum and Dad could get me, she read the letter and had a look at the photos. I was really excited, and I couldn't wait then. I couldn't wait to get there. I didn't feel scared then, just excited.

In November 1985 Link-Up met Kim Chapman and her mother at Strathfield Station to accompany them on Kim's first trip home. In order to have more time to talk over what was to come, the party stopped at a motel at Bathurst for the night.

We went out for a very nice meal, and we were talking about it, how I felt. I went home [to the motel] very tired and excited, had a good sleep. I got up in the morning, felt all right till we got to the sign. Then I was very scared. Nervous and very fidgety. I felt like running around and going away. Then when we got to there, I thought we were going straight there, but we didn't. Link-Up went round to see if Vicky was home, then they picked me up and took me round there. When we got outside her house I froze, didn't want to go, didn't want to move. As I was getting out of the car, this little head popped round the corner, and it was my little niece. I walked in and she just walked up to me and gave me a kiss, and it was all right them. Just showed her the photos and talking, we got on really well. The hard part was just getting in the door.

Then the next thing was going up to Nan's which was a lot more nerve-racking. Two cousins came round, then they went round to Nan's and it was time to go there. Vicky walked straight in, then I had to walk in, and there she was. Then I met my other sister, then all the family. I was all right after I got in there, it was all right after a little while. It was good.

Actually there wasn't much conversation until Link-Up and Mum had left—that's when we started talking. Nan was asking me questions, where I came from and things like that. Then other family would drop in. After everyone had left and we'd been talking for a while, Vicky said there was another cousin who wanted to meet me who'd made afternoon tea. That was Sharon. So we went round there. She was very very nice, and I felt very relaxed there.

The only person who really made me nervous was Uncle Tommy, being drunk and that didn't help. When he'd look at me he'd say, 'Oh Joanie. My Joanie's back.' That didn't make me feel very good. Apparently he was very close to her [Kim's mother]. Every time he'd look at me he'd start to cry. Then Nan came round. We were all sitting round in the lounge room, all the kids, having a good time.

The Toomey family (left to right) Vicky, Carl, Rhoda, Kim and Mrs Mabel Toomey (Kim's grandmother), 1987

Next day we all went in to meet Debbie [another cousin]. We picked up Vicky, went round to see Nan, I think, took some photos. And Debbie was the one who had all the photographs. She showed us the photographs and that's when I got the photo of Iris. That was a shock. For a start it wasn't what I pictured, and she was dead. But it didn't worry me until I found out that the photograph was taken just before she died. So I didn't feel too happy about that. Plus—I know that was a photograph of her, but I didn't feel like I knew her the way I wanted to know her. I felt I didn't have any link with her. Maybe because so many years had passed, I thought that wasn't actually how she looked, so I felt very mixed up. A lot of thoughts were going through my head, and I didn't know how to understand them all or cope with them all. I suppose, when I think now, when I think about her, I don't get angry or upset now. I can cope with it. But I know in time, Vicky and them probably will tell me how she died.

When we were coming back, Mum and I were discussing how we were going to find out. I asked Vicky how she died and she went off the subject, she wouldn't talk about it.

On the way back, someone said it would be a good idea to call in on the way to the hospital. So we went in there, the matron showed us round, she was very nice. The place had changed a lot, but if we needed any more help, to give her a ring. I think coming down in the car, I asked Vicky if Iris was buried there. I didn't get an answer. It wasn't till outside the hospital when the photographs were being taken, she said then, 'Would you like to go to Iris' grave?'. I said yes. Excited in a way. But I got a hell of a shock when I got there. I think it was the thing that hurt the most. Then everything else fell in: that she had no right to die, that I had a right to know how she died. I felt very very hurt. I didn't want to know them, any of them. Didn't care less. I just wanted to go away and not have anything to do with them.

Then I think after that you dropped me off at Nan's for a bit. They asked me where we'd been. Vicky didn't say we'd been there. I don't know why she didn't. It was Nan's birthday that day, her seventy-fourth birthday, I think. I gave her a present, and she gave me a big hug and a kiss different from what she'd given me before. Before, it was like a peck, but this time she had a lotta love there. She showed me all the presents that she's got, and after that I just sat down. After that I was going to Vicky's to talk. Went down to Vicky's. On the way down I was angry because I wanted to get close to them, but I felt like they weren't going as quick as I wanted to go. I felt it didn't really bother them if I was there or I wasn't, and I was pushing Joshua's pram. A cousin just came up and pushed me out of the way and said, 'I'll push it.' I felt like saying, 'You can push him any time—I can't.'

That made me angry as well. I got round to Vicky's and we had no time to talk. She was running around doing things. I don't know, when I asked her certain questions, she wouldn't answer. I just felt like they didn't want me there, they didn't want to know me. So when it was time for me to go, I just wanted to say goodbye the way I knew how to say goodbye. But I never got a cuddle or a kiss or anything. She just said, 'Goodbye Kim,' and turned round. When I got back to the motel, I said, 'Right, I want nothing to do with them, they won't tell me anything, I hate them,' and all this. And cried. Mainly the shock of seeing Iris' grave.

I didn't want Mum to say anything, I think eventually I came in by myself to talk to Coral. It felt better talking to a Koori who'd been through the same thing. We had a really good talk. And that changed my feelings towards seeing them again. So next morning, we called round to Nan and she'd been up really early. She was waiting, and I just ran inside and gave her a kiss and said, 'See you, Nan.' And she said, 'Look after yourself and if you're ever up here there's always a place for you. Just call in.' And that was it. It was hard leaving. I didn't want to go, yet I did. Very strange. I felt I should've got a bit more from them. I felt they should've told me more about Iris.

Kim and her grandmother, Mrs Mabel Toomey, 1986

Why didn't they, do you think?

I don't know. I don't know whether it's because they don't want to talk about it. I feel it's because it's the way she died. I feel there's something terrible, the way she died, so they don't want to talk about it. She's different, in a way I can't explain.

ALICIA ADAMS

Alicia Adams, who had grown up at the Bomaderry and Cootamundra Homes, was studying at Bible College when she received a message that her mother, whom she had never met, was looking for her.

When I was there a nurse wrote up to me to tell me I had a mother. At seventeen! I didn't even know. She said, 'Your mother would like to see you . . .' I was real puzzled, I thought, 'I haven't got a mother.' '. . . Your mother would like to see you at Stockton Mental Hospital.' So I said to Mrs Lloyd, that's the Principal, I asked her if I could

Alicia at the time of the interview for *The Lost Children*

go down to Newcastle one Saturday with somebody to see my mother. When we walked there we both were shaking, because we were so frightened with all these people walking round. When I went up to the verandah the nurse comes out and says, 'What can I do for you?'

'Somebody told me that I have a mother here.'

'Oh you must be Alice. Wait here and I'll go and get her.'

So she went and got Mum. Well I didn't call her Mum. And she came out on the verandah. Dear she was tiny. But she came out, stared at me, and I stared back at her. I thought, 'She's not my mother. No way she's my mother.' I went to say hello and she sort of backed away, and she came to me and I backed away. And the more I was backing away, and I didn't know what to do, I was really confused. And I thought, 'No she can't be.' She said, 'I am your mother,' and I said, 'No you're not.' I was really arguing with her. I said, 'I've got my Mum down in Bomaderry.' She was starting to get tears in her eyes and I thought I'd better stop because probably it was hurting her. Inside. I thought, 'Oh well, I'd better accept it.' So I accepted

Alicia and her sister Sally Boland

it and now we get on so well together. To tell you the truth, I still don't really know my mother. We get on well but I haven't quite accepted Mum as a mother. Then a couple of times later I went down to meet her and that made it feel a bit better. We really got to know each other. Every year I go up there to Sally's place, I usually pop in to see Mum there.

Did you ever wonder why you hadn't been told about her before?

I suppose I didn't worry. I just thought, 'Well I never had a mother or a father, why worry? Just forget about it.' Nobody ever told me I ever had a mother or a father. You expected Mum or the other staff [at Bomaderry Children's Home] to be your mum. But I'm quite happy now I've got a mum. I can go and see her, though I still think she doesn't know who I am really. Danny my elder brother got real mad, but I said, 'Look it wasn't our fault that we got put into the Children's Home. Something could've happened to her, Mum and Dad could have been real drunks, maybe they were wise to take us away from them.' So he was really furious, and I think he still resents her a bit. [I don't blame her] because I wouldn't be here today. I'm glad, I wouldn't be a missionary, I could be in the gutter, I could be a drunkard. I was real glad I was put there in the Home.

[Accompanied by Jean Carter, Alicia went to Collarenebri to meet her family in January 1986.]

Last year [I decided to go home]. Since I've changed my attitude to Aborigines, I thought, 'I'd really like to go to meet my real people.' So I rang Jean Carter up and spoke to her about it, and she was thrilled to bits. She said to contact you. I used to criticise them, and when I used to go and visit them I used to hate eating off their plates and drinking out of their cups, I used to really say things when they were drunk. I don't know, the Lord turned me around, and then five people died through the week,

Alicia Adams (right) with Jean Carter. This photograph was taken in order to send to Alicia's family before she visited them at Collarenebri in 1986.

the Lord spoke to me and said, 'I want you to go out among your own people.' I said, 'No, Lord, why me? Can't you pick on somebody else?' He said, 'No I want you to go out there, you have got to go out and love them like I do.' So my attitude towards my people just turned around, and now I can visit them and eat off their plates and it doesn't worry me. I really love my people now.

Well we stayed at La Perouse on the first night and we left early Saturday morning and we got to Mudgee and had lunch and Jean had a rest. Then we went straight on to Collarenebri—it's a long way. We arrived at about eight o'clock at night time, and we went straight to [Alicia's cousin's] place. She said, 'Tomorrow I'll take you out to the reserve to meet some of your people.' So the next day we went out there and we walked into this house, and there's this old lady sitting on a bed, and she knew me straight away. I got a shock! She said, 'Oh you must be Alice. You're like your mother.' I said, 'Who are you?'. She says, 'I'm your auntie, Auntie Nina', and she really broke down and cried. I gave her a photo of my mother and brother. She couldn't stop hugging me all the time, hugging and kissing, and I'm not used to being hugged and kissed. I thought, 'Oh boy, how am I going to get out of this?'. But then I thought, 'No, I'd better sit here and let her do it, give me a hug and kiss.' She's really beautiful, she's really lovely. My heart just went out to her, because she looks like Mum. Same size. And she was calling me 'daughter' all the time. A lot of them came out to shake hands with me, say hello, and I was really thrilled to bits that I had family.

In the afternoon we went to Jenny Munday, she's my cousin too, and she took me round to meet Charley and Victor and Les Adams and all their family, they all live in the town. I've never seen them so dark, and I thought, 'Oh dear, are these really my people? I don't think they're my cousins.' But they accepted me. Les and them were really excited to see me, and they wanted us to have a reunion. I wanted to get to really know them, but I wanted to get home, I didn't want to stay too long. But I was sad I left them because I wanted to get to know them more. And I drank out of their mugs. But some of the houses had all holes in the walls, it was really terrible. I was thinking in my mind, 'Hope I'm not sleeping here tonight.' But Jean said, 'We'll go to a hotel for the night', and my heart was very happy!

Did you find out why you had been taken away?

They just said they [Aborigines Welfare Board officials] just grabbed us and took us. They said the other children used to hide in the bush from the welfare, but they couldn't help grabbing me and my brother because I was only a baby with Mum, and they [the family at Collarenebri] didn't even know where we were going or where we were.

JOY WILLIAMS

Joy Williams had known her mother for several years before learning that her family came from Erambie Aboriginal Reserve, Cowra. With her son Ben she set off to meet them for the first time in 1985.

You never forget [the trip home]. Never forget it. Oh God, even just going down to Canberra. That wasn't too bad because I was still more or less in my territory. I thought, yeah, I can get off at Bateman's Bay and just come back. I knew the whole thing was going to be different. There's not much in my life, there's not very much that I've finished, but this I was determined to. Because I had had enough—I hate the word 'consciousness raising', but I've had enough of that to know that my children had a right to their family. Even if I didn't have the right, my children did. Even if it [Cowra] is RS, and even if it doesn't live up to my expectations, that's where I'm going.

Saw Coral at the bus station, that was reassuring. Going back to her flat, that was nice. No it was better than nice, it was lovely. Nice and calming. I remember I was nervous as a cat on a hot tin roof. And that carpet, I'm surprised if there is any left of it. Just talking to Coral for hours and hours, and I was delaying. Trying to delay the inevitable too. Hoping the morning would never come. Desperately hoping the morning would never come.

I'd had a look at home on the map, and Ben and I had followed the road up, and I had a vague idea where Cowra was. The closer we got to Cowra, of course, was worse. The snow helped—Ben had never seen snow. I had only seen it when I was little, but it was different. No, it wasn't really, because I was little again and it was very much like the car, the Bomaderry car, the welfare car that took us from the Home to the station. I thought, 'Oh God, it's just like a bad movie happening all over again.' And by the time we got to that signpost I was almost suicidal.

'To Cowra'. I would have given anything to turn around. I think I asked her to turn around, or asked her to stop, or something. And then I was asking, who I was going to see? Did they know we were coming?

[The first house Joy visited was that of Gordon and Valerie Simpson, who lived not on 'the mission' [the Erambie reserve] but in Cowra town.]

I had seen that house before. It's funny. I can't quite explain. But I'd seen that house that you and Ben went in first, and I started bawling me eyes out, and Coral was crying too. And it's funny then, I didn't care about how I was crying. It seemed to me there was a subtle change where I wanted to protect her. She had to just about jemmy me out of that front seat.

Oh God, and then Val. Sometimes I think she waited for me to come home. [Valerie Simpson died in 1986]. And her face. That's when I started feeling not ugly no more. It was like I crawled into that house and I walked out. That was a shock having a face put on a body. And

Joy Williams (right) and her great aunt, Val Simpson, on the day they met, 1985

she was nice and warm. All over her, all around was warm. I often think about how they would have felt too. We had half a million cups of tea, and then Val said, 'Have you been up to the mission yet?'. I nearly died. No bloody way. No way! Not going up to the bloody mission. And Coral says, 'Oh, but they're expecting us.' Oh, what's she on about? Oh dear, bloody hell. In the drive into the mission I was still looking around. Couldn't see any kids or nothing, so that's one bubble burst.

And then we went to Janey's. I'm absolutely besotted with that woman. She's lovely. I love Janey. She thought I was too gub [white]. She asked me if I was too gub to come home. They thought I had known [where to come home to]! She gave me a cuddle. She put her arms round me and I've been her faithful companion ever since. Whither though goest I will go. It's like that. It's funny, I never used to touch people very much before, and now I do it all the time. Every time she walks past me she touches me. Well you know, we might be in the middle of tea, and she'll say, 'I love you,' and it feels good.

With Richard [Janey's younger brother] it was different. Richard stood away from me for a while. I understand why and I had to straighten that out because I found it difficult too. I don't know how you are supposed to relate to male cousins, or Aboriginal men for that matter. I got a shock when you told me he didn't drink. I'm lucky with Richard because we can talk to each other. I don't have to stand away from him and he doesn't have to stand away from me any more, and we both understand anger because as the youngest of the family that was taken away, he knows he can't make up for the past. Neither can I, and I think what Richard and I particularly do now is talk about some sort of future for our children.

Paul Behrendt

Paul Behrendt was raised in the Burnside Home, Sydney, after his mother died. As a young man he learned the truth which he had always felt, that his mother was Aboriginal. Now he set out to establish some links with her, her family and her country.

I grabbed every lead that I could, but there were very few of them. I didn't know any Aboriginal organisation at the time, and in fact I didn't know any other Aboriginal people. It was like sitting at a table with lots of jumbled bits of cardboard. The pieces of cardboard were parts of a jigsaw puzzle and it was a matter of putting the pieces together. But you first had to find a definable piece and place it on the table and say, 'I'm going to build round this.'

The first thing I did when I started out was to apply for a copy of my mother's birth certificate but I was informed by the Registrar-General's Office that there was no record of her birth. I then obtained her marriage and death certificates and found out that she was born at Redbank Mission near Coonamble in 1903. I guess that they didn't worry too much about recording the birth of Aboriginal children in those circumstances in those days. What I did find out was that she had a brother, something I never knew before.

I then set out to travel to the north-west area to see if I could find anyone who knew her, but I didn't meet with any success, primarily because when she was in Sydney she went by her father's name of Dawson, while she was known by her stepfather's name of Boney when she lived in the north-west. In Coonamble I was told to go and see a chap named Tony Boney who might be able to help me. However he didn't know anyone named Dawson at all. It seemed for a while that everything would grind to a halt.

Then suddenly a breakthrough came. It happened when I attended a fund-raising at Tranby [Aboriginal College,

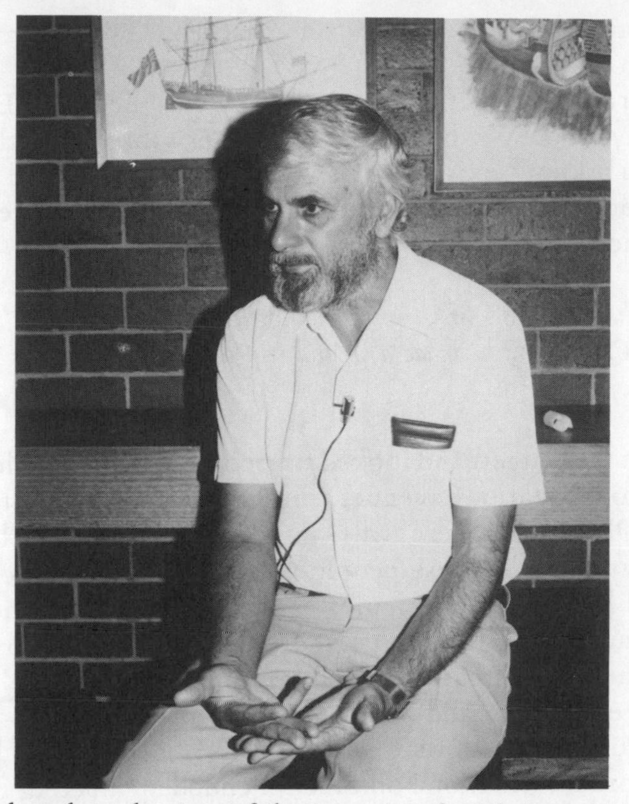

Paul Behrendt at the time of the interview for *The Lost Children*

Glebe]. I ended up talking to a chap called Peter Thompson. A couple of days later I received a letter from him with a note which said, 'Dear Paul, I think this is your Mother.' Enclosed with the letter was an Aborigines Protection Board form that documented the life of Lavinia Boney (also known as Lavena Dawson) while she was in the control of the Board. It was indeed my mother, and I was surprised to find out for the first time that she had a brother. It was my first jigsaw piece. It was the base from which I started to work.

A year later, after a lot of the pieces had fallen into place, I returned to Coonamble to visit Tony Boney.

'Remember me?'

'Yes, you were here looking for your mother's people. Did you have any success?'

'I sure did, and you are one of them. You are my first cousin.'

It transpired that this Tony Boney was the son of Elwood (Sonny) Boney who was my mother's brother—the one I didn't know existed. Tony and his brothers and sisters had lots of kids so I instantly acquired a score of nephews and nieces.

[Paul had made his first trip to the north-west of New South Wales in 1980. In 1982 he made a second trip to find his mother's country and people.]

I went to Walgett and looked up people whom I had learned of through various avenues, might have been able to help me. Of course, there was an initial suspicion, which is understandable. These people were used to people coming in and bleeding their memories and seeing little or nothing in return. But it didn't take me long to establish my credentials, so that matter was quickly resolved. I was accepted more and more and was constantly being introduced to different people. The more people I met, the more information I obtained. I ended up meeting Reggie Murray who was the son of my grandmother's sister.

Only a couple of people [remembered my mother]. The most notable of those was Ivy Green who was her playmate when they were young. They used to live at Dungaleer Station and she took me out to show me the spot where my mother's wurley stood when she was taken by the Protection Board [later known as the Aborigines Welfare Board]. She also showed me the tree in which they built a cubby-house. Surprisingly, some of the wood was still there. She showed me the graveyard where my grandmother is buried. Later, after many visits to the station, she took me into her confidence and showed me an area and said, 'This is the place where our people used to hold their ceremonies. God sent you here because after I go you are the only one who is going to care about this place.' I don't think that the latter part is entirely true, but I doubt if too many people visit the spot or know of its significance.

Did you find out what happened to your mother?

I've heard a couple of conflicting things. What I have established is that her mother died not long after her brother was born. As happened in the old days, she went to live with her mother's brother, Billy Lance, who was according to the old laws, compelled to look after her. There were apparently quite a few people living in the wurley at the time and the conditions were such that it gave the Aborigines Protection Board an excuse to take her into their charge. Not that any excuse was necessary, but on the Protection Board document, it states that my mother was taken by them at her own request 'to get away from

A.P.B. FORM No. 2. A 41/1887 **125**

ABORIGINES PROTECTION BOARD.

No. Date 20th July 1917
Name Boney Lavinia Age Birthday
Place of Birth Redbank, Coonamble Religion —
Reason for Board assuming control of child The girl's own request to get away from Camp life.

Father's name, occupation, and address Alfred [illegible], Carrier address not known.
Mother's name and address Mary Lance, (deceased)
Other relatives Sonny Boney brother at
How many brothers and sisters? [illegible] Station, Walgett
Names and ages 7 years of age.
Been in other situations? No.
Where, and how long?
Further particulars (where living during childhood, and in whose care) [illegible] Camp Walgett.
To which Home sent? Date 1st May 1917
Certificate of admission
Disposal Sent to Mrs Charles Clark, "[illegible]", Coonagendabra. Arrived Sydney March 1921 Child born 3/4/21 at "[illegible]", [illegible] Left for Miss Baptist Pater, "The Hermitage" Private Hospital 20/5/21. Left of her own accord to entered employment of Mr. Thos. [illegible], Bogan St., Parkes 4/4/23.

(Signature) P. W. Alexander
59607 Office Sergt. 3rd Class

The Aboriginal Protection Board committal notice for Paul Behrendt's mother, Lavinia Boney, 1917 camp life'. I have learned that this was absolutely untrue.

My mother didn't go to Cootamundra, probably because she was already about thirteen years old and that was considered old enough to be 'put out to service'. She was taken to a property called Wirrabilla which was near Collarenebri, and nearly 100 miles [160 km] away from her family, where she worked as a housemaid.

I went out to Wirrabilla and had a look at the old homestead, which is still standing but is now used as a storehouse. Even so, you can still picture the grandeur of it all. The kitchen is dilapidated but still intact with its original fuel stove. It would have been the one that my mother learned to cook on. You could see the outline of what were once splendid landscaped gardens, with the scraggy remains of once-splendid palm plantations and manicured lawns. The paling gates are in disrepair but you could still feel the opulence that was there. But most of all, you could feel the presence of people—Koori people.

She worked there for about four years and then became pregnant—to whom we do not know. She was sent to Sydney to have the baby of whom there is no trace. The 'disposal' part of the form states that from there, she was 'transferred' into the services of a woman that ran a private hospital in Parkes.

RICK MCLEOD

Rick McLeod had met an Aborigine in a Brisbane pub who encouraged him to look for his family. Meanwhile his mother June McLeod [Lawson] had already met up with Link-Up in connection with her daughter Pauline McLeod (see pp. 108-110]. In July 1986 the McLeods began to search for the last of the missing children: Rick. In September, just after speaking to Mrs Lawson, Link-Up received a call from the Department of Community Welfare, Adelaide, asking for help in tracing the family of a Rick McLeod. Rick was contacted at work in Brisbane, but it was a few minutes before anyone realised that Mrs Lawson and Rick McLeod were mother and son.

Well I got a phone call from Link-Up on the Tuesday morning. They rang me up and said, 'We're looking for a person called Rick McLeod. He used to be in the army.'

'Well I used to be in the army too.'

'What's your mother's name?'

'Ruby June McLeod.'

'No, we've got a June Lawson here.'

'Well that's not her name, her name is Ruby June McLeod.'

'No, we'll have to go through this file here.'

And he went through the file and buggerised round for a minute, came back and said, 'Oh, I was only talking to her five minutes ago. Her name is June Lawson. But I've got some bad news for you.'

That was when [I learned] Dad was dead. I accepted that. I'd known deep down that he was already dead. And he said, 'Your mother's under a different name, she's known as Lawson.' And he gave me a phone number and I was really rapt. He said, 'Do you want to ring her up, or will I?'. I said, no, I'd ring her up. It'd taken me this long finding her. So I rang up immediately and reversed the charges. It went beep beep beep beep. I remember the switchboard saying, 'Reverse charges call from Brisbane, from McLeod. Do you accept?'

'Yes.'

'Do you know who this is?'

'Yes.'

'Oh son.' Which has always stuck. She said, 'Son' and had a big cry on the phone. That was quite good. Had a bit of a chat, bit of a natter. Mum asked me if she was a grandmother. I asked why? She replied that the others hadn't any children. So I asked her if she was sitting down as she was a grandmother not once but four times. She was ecstatic.

That was about the end of the conversation, that first day I rang up. I rang back that night, and she was too busy down at the pub celebrating, so I found out later. Anyway, next day I rang up, same time, 11 o'clock, and she said, 'I'm very glad you rang up.'

'Why's that?'

'I thought it was just a dream. It's great to hear your voice again.'

That's when Link-Up organised the trip down, and I found out that I had another sister, Pauline. That was really exciting. Well we got funded through Link-Up to go down, and we arrived there at about five o'clock in the morning, the four kids, Janece and Bobby. [Robert had come to meet and stay with Rick and his family a fortnight earlier.] We drove down overnight, itching to get there. Before I left I rang up and told Mum not to die in the meantime, twenty-four years is a long time. Just my luck she'd kick the bucket or something and I wouldn't bloody see her! Got there at about five o'clock in the morning. They'd stayed up till about two o'clock, but we still woke them up, and they were absolutely buggered. I said, 'Come on, no good you just bloody laying in bed sleeping. We've been separated too long. Now come on.' Got her out of bed, big hugs and kisses, kids running round the flat.

Rick (left), Bobby (centre) and Michael McLeod on the day they met in 1986. They had been separated for 23 years. (See front cover photograph showing Rick and Bobby with their cousins in 1963)

It was quite good, quite joyous. Michael [youngest brother] was there, it was excellent. When Mum got up I gave her a big hug and a kiss, she was in tears. It was the strangest feeling, but I felt as if I'd known her all my life. As if I'd been away only a few weeks. It must have always been there in my thoughts. She was exactly what I expected, even though I had photos. There was big hugs and kisses, then she shoved me aside and grabbed hold of her grandkids. And Janece, she was more happy about them! I was quite elated. She was . . . everything I expected. It was great. Excellent.

Then we were all sitting round the house getting a bit nervous, because Link-Up was going to bring Pauline over. I remember she rang up and we had a bit of a chat over the phone. Then Michael and I went out with the kids. We had a bit of a chat. He was so nervous he couldn't even hold a cup of tea. When we came back, Pauline was already there. Big hugs and kisses again, and then Rachel [Pauline's eldest sister, also separated but returned several years earlier] came thumpin' up the stairs and there was

Rick and his mother, June Lawson, with Rick's children, on the day they were reunited in 1986

another big happy reunion. It was good.

Later we drove round to Auntie Eunice's and said g'day to her. Apparently they used to look after us when we were kids. She was in tears. And Uncle Victor came round, he must have been woken up from shift work, and the only thing he said to me was, 'You haven't changed much except you've got a big fat gut.' That was it, that's all he said to me. That made me feel really welcome. That was it until I saw him again at the barbecue on the Saturday, and it was brilliant.

It was Rachel's birthday, and as it fitted in to the family reunion, we all went over there for the barbecue. It was tremendous. Met all the rest of the family who came up from Jervis Bay and Nowra—where I was brought up from, and didn't know they were there. I was feeling really elated. It was nice to feel that everything slotted in. It was like a big jigsaw puzzle, it all fell into place. And the kids, they were just rapt, as if they'd known everyone all their lives.

Jeanette Sinclair

Jeanette Sinclair was raised in New South Wales by her white grandmother, although her mother lived in Perth. By the age of twenty-seven she was studying at Tranby Aboriginal College in Sydney. All she knew about her Aboriginal family was her mother's name.

I remember the first day I was at Tranby. I'll always remember that day. I was terrified about going and I thought I'd better not dress up too much because they will think I'm a snob, but I can't dress down too much otherwise they will dress nicer and they will think I'm an idiot or something. I didn't know what to do and so I wore shorts. Shorts, a T-shirt and a pair of sandshoes. I was skinnier then!

I came to class and I was early. First time in my life that I've been early I think, and I was so nervous. I'm sitting in the corner and everybody started coming in and they all sat in the other corner, and I was in this other corner all by myself. And the reason why they hadn't come and sat next to me is because they thought I was the teacher you see, so they were all standing away. And they were talking about their family and where they come from and that really upset me. I can remember that. Like, a lump in the throat job. I thought I was going to cry, thought I better go to the toilet and wash my face. They were all yapping, saying, like, 'What's your name?'. 'Oh I'm your cousin.' 'I'm bla bla's son.' And every bastard there was related! I was thinking to myself, 'I'm the only odd bastard out.' I know nobody, I can't tell nothing. Anyhow, they eventually came over to me and asked, 'What do you teach?'

'I don't teach anything, I'm a student, just like you are.' And they looked at each other, looked at me, thought it was a bit weird, and then I think they thought to themselves, 'I bet she is.' And they said, 'What's your family name?'

I said my married name: I didn't know how the system worked, did I? I hadn't been educated, not the black way and so I said 'Mannix'. And they're scratching their heads.

'We don't know no blackfeller named Mannix.'

'Oh no, that's my ex-husband's name.'

'What's your mother's name? That's what we want to know.'

'Oh, Collard.'

And one of the women who'd been staring at me, making me feel very uncomfortable, she said, 'I thought I recognised you: you gotta be one of my cousin's kids. What's your mother's name?'. I said, 'Doreen.' And she said, 'Yes, she's my cousin.' It just fell into place like that.

And she rang up that day. She couldn't get hold of my Mum, she got hold of my mother's cousin who is, like, head of our family because all the elders have died and he would have been the only one to know that she'd had children that were taken away because my auntie was actually a lot younger than my mother, so she didn't know that my mother had had us three kids. He wouldn't give her the number straightaway, he hung up and rang back and gave us the telephone number for us to ring that night. This is all on the first day at Tranby! I couldn't wait for Tranby to finish that day. I couldn't get out quick enough. I went home but I couldn't ring up. It was, like—what do I say to her? And I was going out with this guy at the time. I had to get him over here to help me with that telephone call. He was really good, he came straight over. He sat there and helped me with questions to ask. It was terrifying, exciting and horrible.

I asked first, I said, 'Are you my mother?'. What else could I say? And she was in the middle of a meeting—can you believe it—with about forty people at the table and the telephone had been brought to her in this room with forty people. Not the best place to have a conversation. I couldn't say 'Hello Mum,' because it might not have been her, and I said, 'Hello, are you my mother?'. I can laugh about it now. And I can still remember Anthony going, 'No, no, don't say that, it sounds stupid.' And she went quiet for a minute, and she said, 'Who is this?'. And I said, 'It's Jeanette,' and she says, 'Jeanette.' And I knew straightaway that I was her daughter. She says, 'Where are you?'. She says, 'I can't talk now, I'm in a meeting, I can't talk you now.' But it wasn't emotional, it was very clipped, closed, unemotional sort of thing. And to hear her voice, I am trying to get an image out of her voice of her face, and I said I would ring back and we hung up.

I felt terrible. I felt bad, I felt really bad. Just cried and cried. It wasn't what I was hoping for. I used to have those dreams all the time about finding my mother and how we'd rush into each other's arms and cuddle and kiss and all that sort of stuff. But the biggest impression of that telephone call was that it was a business telephone call, that's what it felt like. And I nearly didn't ring back the next night because it was nothing like I hoped it would be. Because she was so clipped on the telephone. 'I can't talk now' sort of thing. I thought, 'Maybe she doesn't want to talk to me. Maybe it's a big shock to her, she doesn't want me back, and maybe I am something she wants to forget about.'

But I rang back the next night, Anthony in tow again. Anyhow, the second conversation wasn't very good either, even when there wasn't somebody there. I didn't know what to say. What do you say after not seeing somebody for twenty-seven years? It was just no good. And so I thought to myself, before I rang her, I'll get her address, maybe it will be easier for me to say what I want to say in a letter. So I got her address and I gave her mine, and it was the best thing I did. I stopped ringing her because it was no good on the telephone and I started writing. I wrote for six months, back and forth, between her and I, telling her some things that had happened to me.

She [replied and] told me about her life then, with her family, my brothers and sisters. They all knew about me. I didn't know about *their* existence until my Mum said I had brothers and sisters and their names and how old they were and everything, and what they did. And that's basically what we talked about on the telephone. And I told her that she had a grand-daughter and she said she knew! She had known I had a daughter and had bought—this kills me—a cot, pram, baby clothes. She'd sent a telegram over by my father but he didn't send it on to me. But I don't know if I could have handled going back then. Yeah, I don't think I was strong enough emotionally. I think he may have done me a favour in the long run, because I don't think I could have handled it. It's a hell of a lot to take in, and I'd just had a kid, and I was only a kid myself.

So we built up a kind of picture of each other, through these letters over six months. And she sent photographs also, and through the letters I could build up an impression of what she was like inside, and the photographs supplied the outside picture.

The trip to Perth was the worst experience of my life, the worst. I remember Coral saying something to me about, as you get closer to home you get younger and younger and it's true. Jesus, it's true. I was twenty-five, then I was twenty and I was fifteen and then I was ten. By the time I got to WA I was literally the age I had been when I left. I couldn't function. Sharmane had to organise everything.

As soon as I got to WA I rang TAA [now Australian Airlines] to make bookings to get out. I just couldn't cope with it. It was just too highly emotional. I felt totally vulnerable to anything that could possibly happen and I didn't know what anything was. So I wanted to get out. And my Mum, I'd actually rung her to let her know we were coming. She said, 'What time will you be at the bus terminal?', and I said, 'Well we're not quite sure what time the bus comes in, so I'll ring you when we get there.'

I got there at seven o'clock in the morning thereabouts, and I couldn't ring her. I thought, 'It's because I'm dirty, that's why I can't ring her. I've got to have a shower.' So I said to Sharmane, 'Find us a motel.' So she got us into a taxi, got the bags in and told the taxi driver we wanted a motel, reasonably priced please. Got us into a motel, she booked us in. I went upstairs, had a shower and passed out, cold as anything, just passed out. She sat up and watched telly. I woke up and she says, 'OK, ring Nanna and tell her we're here.' It was about two in the afternoon.

'No I can't do it.'

'Why not?'

'I'm not ready yet, I'm not ready.'

'How about an ice-cream?' She'll do anything for an ice-cream, right?'

'Ok, we'll have an ice-cream first, then we'll ring up Nanna.' But we had to go all the way back into the city for an ice-cream. So back to the city we went, walking round from shop to shop trying to use up time so that I didn't have to ring her up. But Sharmane snuck off and rung my mother and told her where we were staying. We got back to the motel and there she was!

It was really strange. We got out of the taxi and there she was and I wasn't prepared for this. I knew who she was from photographs but I still wasn't prepared. Even though I knew why I was coming, I don't think that anybody can be prepared for that situation. I wish I'd had someone to hold my hand. I mean, it was great that Sharmane was there, but somebody older, it would've been a great help. Although if I hadn't had Sharmane, I'd never have met her. I would've run away from the situation, I'm quite certain about that. But she was great. She said hello and it wasn't like mother and daughter or anything, but a couple of old friends. Because of the letters and telephone calls, we knew about each other. On the telephone there would be long gaps of silence where we didn't know what to say, but [now] we could chat about the family and that, it was comfortable. Mum spoiled Sharmane, because Sharmane was what I was at that age, and she still is spoiled by Mum. I suppose it's because Sharmane is the child that I was and she lives my childhood through Sharmane, the loss of it.

How long did you stay in Western Australia?

Ten days. It was too long. I felt after five days I wanted to go but I desperately didn't want to offend her. And

Jeanette and her daughter Sharmane

so I stuck around for the agonising other five, agonising because it was just too much more emotion and too much information to take in, emotional information, and I was exhausted after five days.

I stayed [with Mum] because I was not in the financial situation to stay in a motel. I stayed with her for those ten days, but I tried to make myself scarce the last five days without making it obvious. It was great I was there for Mother's Day for the first time in my life. It was great finding I had all these brothers and sisters, that was really good. And that my place had been kept for me. That to me was very strange. Coming back to a house thinking I have so much to adjust to, and my brothers and sisters have an equal amount to adjust to—that suddenly they have got a sister. Well, it wasn't sudden, they'd always known they had an older sister called Jeanette, so when I fronted up on the doorstep they all ambled round, I mean literally ambled. It wasn't exciting or anything new. I'd always existed, so they said, 'G'day Jeanette.' That blew me out. I didn't know how to take it. My place had been literally kept for me all those years and I just slotted right in. It was a really, truly brother-sister relationship. At first it freaked me out a bit because they were so casual about it. But I think Tranby had given me enough education to be able to put things in a lot better perspective. I just thought, 'Well, I'll go with it. Just calm down, go with it,' and things just fell into place.

Was there anything else that was really strange to you?

Yes, I'm fastidiously clean and ordered. I like things clean and I like things ordered. It's from a mixture of being pumped in my head through the Homes and through my white grandmother. Well my mother is the opposite. She just couldn't give a shit: there's more important things in life than cleaning a house, and that's being with your family, enjoying yourself, going visiting and having a yarn, whatever. That to me was strange, first off. That made me uncomfortable. But I went over there with one clear notion in my head and that was I wasn't to judge. I just had this feeling that to judge her would push her away from me. And the whole idea of going over there wasn't to judge or to find out what happened, it was to find her, and in finding her, find myself. So the first night was hard, very hard but after that I came to terms with it and I laugh about it. You see, that's just Mum. But it was very hard at first because of all those things that had been pushed into me as a child. It was very hard for me to let go.

NANCY DE VRIES

Nancy De Vries had learned her mother's name when she was about twelve, but it was not until she was in her fifties that she learned of the whereabouts of a woman of her mother's name. She arranged to make contact with her as soon as possible.

Now I blame myself for what has happened. Because after fifty-two years I was so anxious that my mother would accept me with open arms, put my arms round me and be happy that she'd found me again. I got on to the Salvation Army Missing Persons. They went round to see her. I believe that Ruby got very upset and was shaking and was crying and denying, she didn't know any woman that'd be looking for a mother. She was crying and shaking, didn't want to know, didn't want to see me.

So I went up to her. Used a friend of mine to go with me because she was a health worker in that area. She and I went out there and I had sunglasses on and I said that my name was Mary Harris. Zelma introduced me as Mary Harris and we sat down and we were talking about living conditions and some woman named Shirley, and we were talking and talking. Ruby got up, I was sitting next to her, and she walked out of the room, and she came back in and sat down and I whipped off my sunglasses. I have light-coloured eyes for a Koori. And she looked at me and she was startled. She looked at Zelma and she said, 'Ah, have you heard from that lady who's trying to find

Nancy de Vries and her daughter Megan

her mother?'. I just looked at Ruby and smiled because I knew bloody well she knew who I was. She knew. She sent me round to her daughter Vally. So I went around, and as I walked through the door of Val's house she nearly dropped her crocheting. She looked at me very suspiciously as if I was going to cause a lot of trouble. When she invited me to sit and we sat down, we were talking and I was telling her about my Ruby, about how I'd heard that perhaps her birthday was in June, how old she would have been, all these things. Not once did Vally say, 'No no that couldn't be my mother.' All Vally did the whole time was to say, 'Mmmm.' But she never once said no, that cannot be. Both Val and Ruby said to me, 'Will you come back again?', and I said yes. But I didn't go back because I thought I can't intrude into this woman's life. This woman has got to say to me, 'Nancy, I want you.' I think being a mother helped me to be strong about this and not make a fuss and disrupt the whole family. I thought that for a woman to lose her child fifty years ago, and suddenly be confronted by this middle-aged older sort of woman coming and saying, 'Mummy,' I think it'd be a pretty big shock to her.

When I didn't hear from her, it was after that I met the Link-Up people. Finally I was with people who had the same experiences as me, who knew what it was like to search for your identity. A lot of them didn't even know what it was like to search for your identity. A lot of them didn't even know that they were Aboriginal until they started to query about their parents, so some of them had lost their identity totally. I hadn't, I identified as an Aboriginal person, I was lucky I hadn't lost that. But I didn't know who I was, I didn't know where I fitted into the society, I didn't know where my people were from. But here were a whole lot of other people. We could sit, we could talk, we could cry, we could laugh about things that had happened, and nobody took any notice. Everybody was supportive, everybody knew that if you cried . . . The first couple of Link-Up meetings I came away with the most violent headache because it was emotional—this sudden ability to be able to be me. I knew how they were feeling. Everybody [else] got sick of hearing how lonely I was, how lost I felt. Here were people that didn't give a damn [about hearing it many times], *they* knew what I was talking about. They accepted it, if you cried you cried, and there was always someone there to put an arm around you and hold you and say, 'Don't worry, we're here.' This had never happened to me in my life.

So I was at college. Link-Up went to her place and she wasn't there, but I think they had doubts [that it was the right woman]. Now I've heard that her upbringing was very strict, that it was a shame, a shame to have a child out of wedlock, more so with Koori people.

As the woman thought to be Nancy's mother refused to acknowledge her, a plan was formed to visit her again, and to leave with her a letter addressed 'To Whom It May Concern'. The letter asked the real mother to get in touch with Link-Up or Nancy when she felt ready to do so.]

When finally Link-Up got in touch with her she didn't respond, she just stared away. She accepted the letter, the family read the letter. And they started to question her then: 'Come on Auntie Rube, what's your big dark secret? What's in your past?'. She would not answer them yes or no, 'I'm not talking about this.'

In May [1986] I was in mid-semester, working my little butt off trying to cope with study after forty years. Then [I got a message that] Ruby would like to see me. Well, I raced up to the office, tried to tell my principal lecturer, I was crying because I was happy, I was emotional, I just can't explain how I was, I just know I was feeling pretty crazy. I blurted out something about my mother wants to see me. I went off on cloud nine, I told them I was going away.

I couldn't get on the bloody bus, I couldn't get on the train. I've never flown in a plane, but I would have got on that. But I couldn't get on a plane. Finally I got on a seat, I was booked on the Monday. I started my journey.

I didn't know how far the town was away. The nearer I got there the more apprehensive I became. I wanted the bus to stop, I wanted to get off in the middle of nowhere. Because going home is pretty terrifying, I was on my own. When I got there the first thing, Dolly took me round to her place and she asked me did I want to wait till the morning or did I want to see Ruby then? What a stupid question; but I said no I want to go and see her now, and round we went. It was the first time that I'd ever really had a chance to have eye to eye contact with Ruby. I think we sat there for twenty minutes just looking at each other.

It wasn't the reception I expected. I expected her to greet me, put her arms round me and tell me 'Welcome home', or 'I love you.' But it didn't happen that way. Ruby kept on saying to me that she didn't have a daughter, she only had a daughter but she died. Later Dolly told me that she'd gone into Crow [her son's] room and said, 'What do you think?'. He said, 'Well one thing's for bloody sure, she's one of us.' They were talking a little while longer, and then he said to Dolly, 'You get out there and look after my big sister.' So Crow was the first one to accept me. But he didn't tell me! Whether he's a male and males are a bit shy I dunno, but . . .

So I went back and I was pretty down. Ruby kept on saying, 'I wouldn't give my child away', and I kept saying, 'But I know that my mother didn't give me away.' [She said] 'I would have tried to find you', and I said, 'Yes I believe that, but the people had moved, and I'd been moved, and it's pretty difficult when people start moving to find out, especially for someone from the country.' I said, 'But I don't care, it doesn't worry me, it's all in the past. I'm not here to be judgmental, I'm here to know if I've got my family right.'

So I stayed one night with her at Auntie Glad's place. I kept on saying things, and I noticed that Gladys would look at Ruby and Ruby would sit there, very tough old lady, and wouldn't answer. I felt there was something there, but she wouldn't let go, she couldn't let go. I think perhaps she may have resented me coming in changing her quiet little world into something that could have been threatening. These are just my assumptions, I try to look at it [this way]. I *know* Ruby is my mother. I *know*. And nothing that Ruby ever does or says is going to change my mind. I know I am her daughter, I know she is my mother. I looked at her hands and I saw my hands. I looked at her eyes and I saw my eyes. When people up there can come up to me and start consoling me over the death of my husband and then suddenly realise that I'm not Ruby that they're talking to, it only strengthens that I know that Ruby is my mother. When old people come into the [Aboriginal Medical] Service and have their blood pressures taken by me, and we talk, and they call me Rube—I know that Ruby is my mother. When people walk up and say, 'Oh, I thought you were Ruby', I know that Ruby's my mother. When my sister, my beautiful sister looked at me, she said to me, 'I cannot get over how much you look like Mum when she was young.' When I said I would have loved to have had somebody that was mine other than my kids at my graduation, she can say to me, 'Will your little sister do?'—that's good enough for me. The tragedy of it is, I think, after fifty odd years of me looking for her, that poor old darling cannot come out and say, 'Welcome home.' I think she thinks I'm angry with her, I think she thinks I blame her. But I don't blame her, I blame the system that was in then, I blame society, no way do I blame my mother.

I'm still living in hopes. It's funny after all these years of being away that I'm working close by. I had no idea that I was going to work there, and that's what I say, there's a reason in your life for everything.

THREE

Reflections

Jean Carter

One of the things I was really aware of in the community, was they all had close friends that they'd grown up with. They'd talk about things they did in their schooldays, and most of them had stories to tell, and there'd be someone in the room to say, 'Do you remember this?' and you felt really left out on that sorta stuff. That's one of the things you're cut off from, eh. In a Koori conversation, that's one of the things, 'Do you remember this?'. Sharing times. And knowing who your family are. People come up and say, 'I'm your cousin, I'm such and such', and you get really confused.

I still think I'm learning things. I think that before I felt comfortable in Wreck [Bay], I started to feel *more* comfortable and part of the family and all that, in the bean [picking] paddock. Didn't do it very many times, but it must have been the first time I went picking, and me brothers were in the drills, and everyone was really happy and they used to be joking all the time. They always had people laughing. And I felt that was the real feeling. It was really good, becuase we were all working, there was more of the family working. There would have been Chicka, Sago, Sally, Cyril and Andy. It was real good. We had tents, and all around together. I think that was when it all started to come together. That's why I think I like going down the coast still, the boys made it really easy for me to mix with them down there, with the families and that. It was just their nature. Sally really loved Wreck Bay.

What do you think you had missed out on most?

One was knowing where I fitted in my family. There was certain things that my brother said that I should have took notice of, and because there wasn't that authority there for me, in my growing up, I disregarded them, and didn't recognise their authority. And I guess I really needed that at that time. I resent all the years I missed, in the family. I just went down the coast last week, and I was thinking, 'Dear it would be lovely down here now if me brothers were still around.' I was going to a turn-out down there at Moruya, a talent quest, and I was thinking they would have loved that, they would have been up on the stage—this is me thoughts going all the time. 'Cause when I drive down that way they always come to me real clear. They were saying, 'Now the contestants, they're not up here yet,' urgin' them to come up. And I was thinking, 'Ah, dear, my brothers'd be the first to go up. Tommy would've loved it.' And that sort of stuff you know. I cry easy about it. It was like sorta, what it did to them, too, you know. They were members of a big family, and knowing how much importance Aboriginal people place on the family, what they must have went through . . .

How long after you had been at Wreck Bay did you start getting involved in community work?

I think I was only about twenty-six, twenty-seven, about five years after. I was Secretary of the Progress Association, 'cause I could write, I suppose, knew a bit about how to run a meeting, must've been from school days. And I thought they didn't know very much about how a meeting should be run. That was first. Then I got on a Country Women's [Association] thing, they came there to Wreck Bay. Next thing I was working in the preschool there for about five years, and I started reading a lot more then, reading Aboriginal stuff. Then I went to a few meetings, nothing really political. Went to Canberra, couple of meetings up there, Family Planning Association thing.

How do you feel about the people who actually took your family away?

I can't condone what they did. That was something that the government wanted, and I think we were all manipulated by the government. It's sorta like, I can never bring me family back, no matter how much hate and sorrow that I feel, I can't bring me family back as we were. Before, I couldn't even talk about it. Not openly about things as I can now. I could never ever say me mother's name, to say 'Mum', I used to just break down. So I guess the memories are all still there, and they're all good memories of them, of Mum and Dad and the boys. Maybe because I'm getting older too, there must be some time in your life when you come to terms with things. You know that things have gone. And I put it down to what had happened in my life. I haven't got aggression now like I had, 'cause I've had inner healing, I've been prayed for and that. I know a lot of stuff came out of me that wouldn't have come out of me otherwise.

Is the fact that most of your brothers and sisters are no longer with you now, because they were taken away?

Yes, I really feel that. The importance Aboriginal people place on the family, it's the first and foremost thing. When you're stripped of that, I reckon you maybe don't care, lose all your . . . It's sorta like a shame thing, eh. I guess they went through a lot of that. And feeling really powerless, and what could they do. And they drank, and died really early. They all died in their forties, all the boys except Sago. Wherever they went they had close friends and that, but maybe they were searching too, looking for that family. They just didn't care, really. I used to say to Andy he could've been anything, he was that brainy. But he just didn't care. Just wanted to be with his mates all the time, and I think that's the thing they'd missed out on, and they were searching for it. I like to be around Koori people all the time but they've gotta be close friends. I couldn't sorta—I don't know what the word is—move from family to family and feel really like belonging, even if you were related—but not belonging. When I see that close-knit family thing, I feel really comfortable in that family group. Maybe it's just a continual search.

Could you tell us a bit about Jilimi, the women's organisation which you run?

As I look back, it was a bit of a bold step. I think over the years, because I was involved in different organisations, my experience built me up to that day when I knew I could have a go. I knew I could do it. Understanding too, respecting Aboriginal people, and not just giving them something, 'Oh, I think this is good for you.' It wasn't to have a women's centre because white women were getting it—it was just that there was a need for Aboriginal women, I felt, going on my past experiences as a health worker, that made me think about it.

It started off getting Koori women to come in and have their Pap smears, and once they could see and hear of Koori women dying, being diagnosed and being told they had three months or six months to live. Koori women back ten years ago, very few of them would use the doctors, but they'd go if you went in with them, or talked to the doctor first. Over the years different doctors used to say, 'Why don't Aboriginal women come in for a check-up six months after they've had their babies?'. When I left the Health Commission in a huff I had it in the back of me head that there was something I should have done about that, and I hadn't. Then when I got that six-months job with the Women's Resource, I first heard that there was Aboriginal women doing Pap smears at Liverpool. I went up there and I had a look at the Centre, met the women there, I came back and we were going to go for a little clinic-type room in the Women's Centre there, and we couldn't get any approval from the Council to do any renovations. There was a lot of squabbling and that going on with the Directors. I thought, 'Koori women couldn't work in this sorta atmosphere. Koori women wouldn't even come.' So I went out for a place of our own, and the submission went in, and the girls at the Centre showed me how to do it. It was approved, and that's when we moved up to Berry Street [Nowra].

In that twelve months, the last half was spent going

to meetings and getting support from women's groups to have the CEP [federal government job-training program] on-going. We didn't, but we got some money to keep the building, and for about three or four months I worked without pay, went to meetings on me own steam to get the funding, went to the Women's Co-ordination Unit, had a big mud-brick building designed by an Aboriginal woman. Never got any money, but the plans are still there. That's something that I'm going to see happen.

There was 600 visits by women, 200 and something by kids, and 300 and something by men, in six months. Fifty-eight representatives of different organisations have come through the Centre. When we put it all together, I was really stunned.

I believe you won an award recently?

Yes, it was 'In Appreciation for Services to the Community' [by the Warragal Aboriginal Association, Sydney].

But the time I feel really good is when we get all the Link-Uppers together. That's a family on its own, eh. You don't have to sorta explain, you can sit in silence and communicate, it's good when you can communicate like that. The right words are not there to express it, and when you put words to certain feelings you have, it's just not the same. For the time you're there, you're getting an intravenous injection or something. Even though you've got family you can still feel alone, you lock yourself away in your room and that, you never really let your family get that close to you. But Link-Uppers do get that close to you. So you can sorta open up, even though you might not be using words. Like, I've opened up a bit tonight, but if anyone had told me a few years ago that I'd be talking about things like this, I'd say, 'No way!'. That in itself you know, being able to talk about it, that's a healing process, eh.

Another thing that changed it around a lot was when I first heard 'Brown Skin Baby' ['My brown skin baby they take him away', by Aboriginal singer Bobby Randall].

And I heard Marge Tucker [Victorian Aboriginal leader also placed in Cootamundra Girls' Home] say something about her mother, and I was thinking, all these years I was feeling very sorry for meself, had that chip on me shoulder and all that, and I started thinking what my mother must've went through. What I went through would be just a drop in the ocean compared to what a mother'd go through. 'Cause I'm a mother, and—losing your youngest children . . . It's not like it was a death, you bury a child. But when you've got to know your kids are growing up somewhere else, and sometimes you don't even know where your kids are, or what's happening, and what sort of influence people are having on them, those sorta things'd be going through your mind. 'Cause Mum was real strict in her ways, very strict about things like swearing and telling lies. The first time I ever got hit I went, 'Oh geez', and I was nearly knocked to the ground. Real hard hit. I never ever spoke like that again.

You seem to have been able to turn to advantage what you learned while you were away?

Yes, you think about they and us—white people. You've gotta be on your guard. There's something there all the time. They're there, and you're here. Even just shopping, you're more or less on your guard, and you don't let it down till you're back home. Precautions or whatever it is. You know a little bit now, you've more or less been on both sides. You can use the English language, and express yourself in ways you know they like to hear. I mean, I can write a letter and I know that's the way they would talk, but if I was writing or talking to an Aboriginal person I wouldn't use half those words. It's important in submission writing and that, there's certain language you use. So in that way, the education has been an advantage. There's no material gains, I don't value that sort of thing. But I do value how Aboriginal people see me, people I respect, and close friends who are non-Aboriginal people. One thing that really makes my skin crawl is whites who patronise us. You think we're equal and then they'll say a little thing, and it really makes you put your guard up.

Is there any messages you'd like to tell people who've been through all this, but haven't come home yet?

The good thing is to know where you are in the community with people who remember you: those people are good to have around you first, and to give you the information. They know your place, your family. There's nothing worse than to go into a community and think that they've forgotten you, as if you never existed. That was why at La Perouse I stayed close to the people that knew and remembered my family and had good things to say. It might've been just a word here, and ten months later something else is said. You're not looking for a lot of information, but things that reaffirm what you know deep down. Something about your Dad or Mum that you remembered, and someone else will say something that will reinforce that memory.

You don't have to be accepted by everybody, only the ones that are important in your [life] that helps your memory, things that you've got stored back there that will flicker something you remember as a child. They don't say a lot of words, but what they do say makes you feel good. It's not flattery, it's something that's sincere. So the people that start to get near you have to be sincere, and not just say things that will make you feel good. There's something deep in you that will respond to that. Someone said, 'Your Dad never drank a drop of grog in his life.' But I know Dad drank. Some things I didn't know—Dad was real political. [I found out that] he was on the first Aborigines Progressive Association which eventually abolished the Protection Board.

Can other Link-Uppers going home do the same as you, do you think?

Well it depends how your family is seen in the eyes of the community. If people are hostile towards them, they'll be hostile towards you whether they know you or not. I get that feeling about people too.

STAN BOWDEN

What happened when you came in to see Link-Up?

Scared. I was scared when I first come up, 'cause I'd never been to Canberra. The [old] office was a little thing, just a little bit bigger than a toilet. A little dark room, and I can't see properly in the dark, so I couldn't see anything hardly. I didn't know who was who. But I left feeling good in a way, 'cause I found out that Coral Edwards was Gordon Edwards' sister, that I was in the [Kinchela Boys'] Home and was good mates with. Gordon and I used often to talk about the Homes when we come out, 'cause he was in the merchant navy too. So it was a bit easier for me to talk. I talked some more over the phone, then I come back up to Canberra, and then I went to a Link-Up meeting at La Perouse. That was good because I found out there was a hell of a lot that had been through the same thing as me. A lot of times I'd felt like I wasn't the full quid. But after that meeting I felt I wasn't stupid like I thought I was. I felt good because I could listen to what other people were talking about, and there was a lot of similarities to what I'd been through, which I didn't realise. 'Cause I'd never really run into anyone [with the same experiences] since I'd left the Homes, except for Gordon. I felt on top of the world, a high.

The next meeting at Jervis Bay, that's when I really felt that I wasn't what I'd thought I was—not the full quid. There was a lot of other people goin' through exactly what I'd been goin' through, but I'd never been able to talk to anyone about it. Not deep. I'd mention it to the odd people, like the AA feller in Albury, but I couldn't tell him everything. Even now I can't talk about everything. But going to the Link-Up meetings, I feel like I'm getting a battery charged every time I go there. I wasn't stupid,

Stan Bowden and his nephew Jason Monaghan at a Link-Up meeting, 1985

it was just all the stuff that was going on inside me that was makin' me feel that way. I felt like there was other people I could talk to that had the same problem. Every time I went back to Albury, gee I felt good. I was able to talk to Link-Uppers the same way an alcoholic talks to an alcoholic. But then Coral told me that they'd found me sister but she'd left a message that she didn't want to be found [Stan Bowden's older sister, Florence, a former inmate of Cootamundra Girls' Home, who had not been heard of since her marriage]. I felt disappointed in one way. But I felt good in another way that I'd let out what I wished I could've done years ago, but I didn't know how to, or who to.

What's happened in the last year?

One trip Link-Up come down and asked me to do a couple of weeks work experience. Which was good. Bigger office though! I went on a trip with them down the south coast. They met some different ones that were looking for their families. That in itself helped me a lot because I felt again that I wasn't the only one that was lookin'. I felt real good when I went back to Albury. It's hard to explain how good I felt. I was floatin', I think. Then after the two weeks, Coral and Peter sat down and asked me whether I'd like to work with Link-Up. I didn't know what to say. I was that excited. Happy. All the good feelings running through me. At first I said I wouldn't do it because I didn't have the education. They said that I had the qualifications. I was a bit confused then, 'cause I thought, I can write a bit, but I couldn't spell. Coral said, 'You've been split up from your family, that's all the qualifications you need.'

I went back to Albury for a while to think on things, but I think I made me mind up there and then. I had to go back and finish up a few things that I started.

This year I've found out more about family, where I came from, where my mother's been buried, more about me grandparents. I know more about me whole family than I ever did, about meself. I feel relaxed now, I don't feel uptight as if I'm about to get up and walk away like I've always done. It's good workin' with other people. Even though I still think of me sister, now and then, it takes me mind off it. I feel great. I've learned to read and write a bit better, through the TAFE, I'm starting to pick up spelling, writing, everything. I feel like I'm a different man altogether. I can talk a lot now which I couldn't before. About the past a lot more. I fit in better now than I used to—with everyone. Before, when I was drinkin', me family saw me just as a bother. Now, they ring me up and ask me about different things. Me opinion. They would never've done that before.

What advice would you give people going through the same thing as you?

Think positive. Don't run yourself down. Don't go judging yourself. Don't give up. See at first I used to be frightened. Wouldn't say boo about anything. Now I'll always have a little dig. I don't feel like I don't know anything about anything. I know I don't really know that much, but I feel that what I can say can help somebody else. I feel like I can help other people, and I have in a couple of cases. A young feller was going to go and get himself into trouble, but I talked him out of it. That in itself feels good to know. Koories come up and say, 'Where you from?'. I feel good because I can tell 'em everything. From Cowra. That feels good because I know I was born in Cowra, and me mother and father are buried in Cowra. I feel like I come from Cowra. I don't have to go back drunk now, I can talk sense.

I can do things now, make decisions for meself, without relying on other people to help me. I feel more confidence in meself. I can do things without worrying about whether I've made the right decision. No lookin' over me shoulder wonderin' who's lookin' at me. Or wonderin' where I'm going. I can help other people as well as meself now.

What is your work in Link-Up now?

One of the qualifications was that I'd been through the

Stan Bowden (right) with Ian Harris, 1988. Stan and Ian were friends as children at the United Aborigines Mission Home, Bomaderry and the Kinchela Home for Aboriginal Boys.

Kinchela Boys' Home, I got split up from me family. A lot of other Kinchela boys are in the same difficulty as me because they don't like talking to anyone as well, apparently. Well if I was here, a lot of the Kinchela boys talk to me better than they would anyone else. And a lot of other men who have been split up from their families would rather talk to a man who's been through the same thing.

PAULINE McLEOD

A week ago I hit rock bottom. Once again. It was like dreaming the whole thing happened. I thought I really couldn't live with it. It was too much. Everything had finally got to me. I was prepared to go. I couldn't give a shit about living and facing the world again. So I took a whole heap of pills and really was ready to die. The dumb things never worked! I got one heck of a headache from it. As a nurse I knew what was dangerous and I thought, 'Oh well, this could do the trick—but it never did. Woke up three hours later crook as anything. I thought, 'Oh well, my lot in life is not to die yet.' And so, slowly but surely building up confidence in myself to cope with what happened to my family, with what happened to myself, and try to help kids who might be facing similar situations. To try to make people understand out in the world, understand what happened to our family. Should never ever happen any more. To steal twenty-four years of a family's life. People will have to know about it. The Department people. The white people in this country. Even the Aboriginal people who just seem not to see what's happened. To really see that it has happened.

Saw Mum again on the weekend. And it was great. I really feel like a kid trying to learn about a mother. Understand her feelings. Trying to learn about the history of my family. Where Mum comes from, her people, her life, her past. I sat down on Monday morning and said, 'Yeah, Mum, how are you feeling?'. She says, 'Oh still in a daze.' When she told me she loved me this time I didn't feel angry with her, and I really love her back, and I hope she believes me. 'Cause she's so sad still. So, so sad. I think as each member gets to know each other and about our various lives . . . Rachel, she went straight on to a drinking spree, tried to dry out but couldn't. Michael, he was the same. I understand that. I can understand their hurts, their pains, their anguish. I just hope that over the next couple of years, as we get to know each other as a family, that we'll be able to find some real peace. That would be great if we could. It would be absolutely great.

It's going to be all right. I don't say I hope it's going to be all right any more, I know it is. And that is going to be the saving grace for me, and may be I'll be able to be that whole person I always wanted to be. Succeed.

Rachel (left), Pauline and Rick McLeod, Link-Up meeting, Nowra, 1986

The Fortunate One

Hey you!
You fortunate one.
Don't turn your back on me!
Don't say 'I don't belong here!'
Don't judge or criticise me!
Saying that I am no Aborigine!!

Hey you!
You fortunate one.
You heard of our history.
The children stolen from their families.
Mothers not knowing where they could be.
Lost and alone with no identities!

Hey you!
You fortunate one.
You who could never know
Or feel the hurt, the pain, of being lost or alone.
You who were raised by your family at home.
Your people you had always known.

Hey you!
You the fortunate one.
I lived part of our history.
I was a stolen child, taken from my family.
I felt the pain, the hurt, the misery.
One amongst a thousand, searching for my Identity.

Hey you!
You the fortunate one
I am tired of being alone.
You'll have to help me, I can't do this on my own.
To find the way, I'll have to be shown,
You see! . . . I want to come home.

Hey you!
You the fortunate one
Don't turn your back on me!
Don't say 'I don't belong here!'
Don't judge or criticise me!
Saying that I am no Aborigine!!!

Paul Cremen

In what ways was it different from what you expected?

Well actually it wasn't. Let's face it, there's only people and people. When you first go up there, maybe you get a false impression from the lawns and houses you see around the area, and you see a few smashed bottles on the footpaths and grass growing up fences, and you see broken windows and flyscreens hangin' off. At first you think, 'What sort of people are they?'. By about Tuesday afternoon or Wednesday you don't sort of notice that, because it's not really how people keep their houses like, it's the people themselves. It's immaterial and I didn't take any notice of it after that. It's something that strikes you first off, but I never worried about it from then on. I suppose if I went back now, I wouldn't worry. It's just the way you're brought up. They don't have to live any pretensions. They don't have to keep things for appearance sake, because it doesn't make them any better a person or less a person. Which means people are more down to earth, they've got a more real outlook on life. Whereas we do things to keep appearances up. It's a veneer that city people put on. That's what I found anyway. The only thing I feel really sad about is that Mum never got to meet her own auntie. It was the fact that she had died knowing nothing much that I actually went in there [to the Aboriginal Cultural Centre in Nowra].

At the end of that week in Murrin Bridge, I think you said you were not going to wash the car again. Do you still feel like that?

That was utter stupidity. I've thought about that to myself. They [Murrin Bridge people] don't need to keep up the veneer, external appearances, but by the same token it doesn't mean that I have to break down *my* standards. Because I know that I'm Aboriginal, and [other] people know I'm Aboriginal, I've gotta show that you can't judge all by some. You've gotta be sensible. You can't get stupid ideas like, 'Who cares if you run round in [dirty] cars or whatever?'—it's the wrong attitude. We're Aboriginals, people are going to be putting us down all the time no matter what we do, and we just have to show that we're Aboriginals and we're the same as other people. As good, maybe better. I want my children to say, 'I'm Aboriginal and I've made it.' Let them be a credit to the Aboriginal community.

What effect did going home have on your children?

They thought it was funny at first, because they wouldn't have known the difference between an African and an Aboriginal. Actually, they used to laugh at black people on TV. But I think they've got a better attitude now than what they had.

Is it any different now, living in Nowra?

Well I tell everyone I'm Aboriginal. Most of the usual statements are, 'You're just out to get some benefit from some organisation.' I just tell everyone that I am [Aboriginal]. They say, 'You've got no more black blood in you than I've got.' But that's their business..

What advice would you give someone going back to meet their family for the first time?

That's a tough one. Take everything as it comes, don't expect too much or you won't get much. But by the same token, when you get it, absorb it. And treasure it. Because it's a feeling like no other feeling that you'll ever have. It's a sort of a love, because it's family. It's relatives that you've never met. It might not work in every case, but it's someone who's your own flesh and blood.

Sherry Atkinson

I started at Tranby College and that just fitted in perfect. There was so many things that I wanted to know about and I thought if I go to an Aboriginal college I'll learn about my own people. And I did, I learned heaps. Everything sunk in. I think when you really want to know something it doesn't take you long to know it. Now when I look back I think, 'God that was incredible.' But it was something I had no control over, I was just forced into the situation. I'm so lucky that I've come out like I have. It would've been so easy for me, if I hadn't found my parents, to have turned to alcohol, anything, but I've just been so lucky that everything fitted into place.

The second time I met my Dad it was different. I went down by myself, it was really scary. It was when I first started at Tranby, I think the first month and I hadn't learned all that much. Going through that culture-identity shock. So I just went back there and really sussed things out. Stood on the outside and looked in for a while, I just couldn't go inside. Then the next time I went down, the more I got educated about the history of Aboriginals, the truth about Aboriginal history and the things they'd gone through, the more I understood and the more I could relate and let go of all those values that I had.

I used to put myself down heaps, 'cause I used to think, 'Why can't I accept the family, why can't I just change and be a big sister and a daughter and be perfect? Why do I have to be so friggin' value [-conscious]?' Cleanliness: I'm a friggin' fanatic about things being clean. Anything on the floor I'll pick up, and they'll look at me—what is she worried about? I might be at a relative's place, an uncle, and there's a whole heap of washing, I'll go and do it. I won't sit there and just yarn, I have to do something. One of the hardest things is being real truthful. Like, I'm truthful but I won't say something to somebody if it's going to hurt them. Because I had been through so much emotionally and hurt too many times, that I couldn't be nasty and hurt other people. I think that will always be my nature. Like even on this tape there's certain things I couldn't say, I dunno why. And money. I've always had money, and every time I go down home I say, 'Yeah I've got money, let's go down here.' I can't help it, I just like splurging. And I give my uncle twenty dollars and things like that. I used to be a fanatic on budgeting, making sure I had money in the bank, but now, I don't care if I've got two dollars in the bank, it doesn't worry me. It does and it doesn't, not as bad as it used to be. I've changed heaps.

Did you ever feel awkward with your family?

Yeah, you're expected to know who this is and who they are, relations and certain places. I met a lot of people in the Medical Centre the other day and they said, 'Do you know this feller at Echuca?'. Now Echuca's not far from Mildura at all, and I just said, 'No, I don't think so', and she says, 'Oh you come from Mildura, you must know.' I said, 'Oh yeah, I probably met him.' [And yet] I was expected to know heaps, to be so educated. When I said I was going to university they expect me to know everything about maths, the law, be an expert. Because I've been brought up by whites I'm expected to know the white world, and I do, to an extent. You've got the stuff that's unconsciously been put on to you, but that's not good, you want to forget that. So you don't want to be labelled as 'the one that goes to university'.

All the way, it gets me down sometimes. I should go home for two years to settle in. My Dad just wants me to come home and be with him and be part of the family like I should be, 'cause he feels sorry about the things that

I've been through. And so do I want to go, but things just restrict me. That freaks me out bad. I don't think I'm ready emotionally yet to go down there permanently. I've got to sort myself out. And when I'm down there it's never long enough for Dad. He says, 'Oh whata you want to go back for?' It's hard on him and he doesn't understand, he thinks, 'Well you've met me, why don't you want to be with me, don't you love me?' sort of thing. I'm sure that's what he thinks: 'Why aren't you at home where you belong, you've been away long enough.' I'm sure he thinks that but he won't say it. But I think he knows I'll come back when I'm settled.

And my 14-year-old brother, he throws his weight around, he knows that he's the oldest and be the first one to do everything, and when I came back he thought it was good, but he thought, 'Oh no, I've dropped down now.' That was at first and I suppose I slapped him round the ears a bit saying, 'Stop being so cheeky.' Now he's all right because he realises what he can get out of me. But at first he could have punched me one because I was the oldest.

Last year I was really hyper, going to Land Rights marches, really rebelling against society, but now I'm a lot more stable, that urge to change the world and make everything different, will always be a dream of mine.

Is there anything you'll never get back?

My past. That's true. Even though I've gone through an identity change and I feel a lot better, I still get upset over things that I've gone through and I've had to put up with. I just feel like I've really been cheated, cheated bad of my life. It's only now that I can make things change, but I find it hard because I'm still reminiscing about what happened to me, still trying to recover. I don't know if I'll ever recover. One thing I know, I'll never put my kids through what I've been through. And at university I found I was educating people every day. But one thing I realise is your Aboriginal identity, being an Aborigine, the spiritual link with the land our mother, and the relations between all my people will never change. No matter what the white man did or does, it's the spirit and soul he will never take or destroy. Our Ancestor will always guide us and bring us all home both physically and spiritually. I will stand as an Aboriginal woman till the last day and stand strong and proud.

KIM CHAPMAN

Is there a difference between how you feel now, and the night before you met your family?

Yes, I know what they look like now. I know where they live, how they live. The only thing that makes me anxious is finding out about Iris [i.e., about how Kim's mother died]. That's now what I really want to find out, and I don't know how to find out about it, whether I should leave it until they want to tell me. I don't know if they'll ever tell me. Or if I should just find out for myself, but I have doubts about that because I don't want to get a shock again. I don't know how I could cope with that. I'd probably go up there angry and fly off the handle—but I'm dying to find out.

Have you been able to write letters since then?

Yes, I've written my second letter. Today! I'm too lazy to write. I've made phone calls, I've rung Vicky and Vicky's rung me. And I'm hoping to meet her in Sydney when she comes down. But knowing what to say is another [reason why it's hard to write].

Do you think they should write first?

I feel so, yes. I feel I should get a letter or a phone call out of the blue, you know, because I'm pushing myself in having to write all the time. Actually I'm hoping that

Vicky will write to me in Sydney, that'll make me feel a lot better. I'm hoping she just didn't say it. But I feel I'm not as close as I want to be. Actually only a little while ago I got really angry about it all. I put the photo albums away in the place I had in the bedroom and didn't want anything about it mentioned. Sitting at home by myself one day, I just started to think about it. I pulled them out then and I was just looking at them. Then I remembered going home and the conversation we had and I thought, 'It's a lot easier for me to write to them than it is probably for them.' So I thought, 'Oh yeah, I'll get round to writing,' and I felt a bit better about it. I only just wrote today.

Do you feel differently about other Koories now?

I suppose it's become more important to me now, I don't know whether it's because I went home or not. I think it must be, because it never used to worry me before. I used to look at myself as white, but now I do feel different. With nearly every Aboriginal person I've met, there's sort of like a bond there that makes you special, brings you together. You feel a lot more relaxed round that person. And the friendship lasts a lot longer. That makes me feel, for the Aboriginal people, very glad and happy. They're very special people, they're people that have it. I feel we should have a lot more interest taken in the Aboriginal culture. And this has only been recently. Not till I went home and they said, 'There's always a bed here.'

Was your reunion different from what you imagined it would be?

Very different. Very different. I didn't picture them the way they were or the way they lived, at all. It wasn't the way I lived, compared to the things I have. One example was, Vicky said to me, 'Have you travelled?'

'Yes, I've been to Hawaii.'

'Money! You're rich!'

'No, I'm not rich.'

'It takes money to go overseas.'

Things like that. I felt different. I'd had an education—without trying to put them down. I looked around and I saw things that were different to what I had, without trying to be mean or anything. It wasn't what I expected at all. Just mainly silly little things. There's a lot of people in there, a lot of people, all the time. It just felt different. To me it was like everything was for everyone. Everyone shared everything. They shared everything. It wasn't till I saw what they had that I thought—they deserve what I had. To me you feel crammed in, in Nan's house, like, you can't move, and I feel she needs a bit of privacy. I'd love her to have lots of clothes and things like that. But probably the first thing I'd do is get Iris' grave fixed up, for sure. I picture it how I'd like it to be done: I'd want it with a fence round it, so it's private, not stuck right up the end. It means a lot to me to have that done. Some days I think about it all the time, and some days I just don't think about it. I think that the main thing that goes through my head is her and her life, how she lived. That's really why I started to look, for her. But I don't know whether to ask them [natural family], whether it's going to offend them, whether they're going to be angry or not, or whether I should do it by myself. I don't know.

Do you feel very different from the rest of your natural family back home?

I don't know, there's a difference. And there's the ones like, back home, who probably will never get overseas. Just things I take for granted, like going shopping and buying whatever I want. I feel she wasn't like them. I feel I'm there too, and in a way I feel like I've got a goal in my life. I'd like money, and if I ever had money the first thing I'd do is do her grave up, and I'd make sure that they'd had some of the things that I've had. I'd love Nan to be in a nice big bright house with a lovely garden in the front. She probably enjoys having kids round, but I feel that sometimes Gran would like to be by herself, I don't know. And I'd love Vicky to have a place of her own, no worries. I'd just make sure that they'd have the things that I've got, and at least once in their life, all the close ones that they could go somewhere overseas and say, 'I've been here.' That's what I'd really like to do for them. In a way, I feel Nan deserves something better than that, because she's worked her guts out all her life, and she deserves something. So I'll work for that, and for them.

Alicia Adams

Do you feel sorry for your people back home, who never knew where you were?

I don't know. I don't think so—oh it's so hard. I s'pose a lot of the people up there are still resenting what they have done, but being older I thought I'd like to be accepted back into my family—but it can't be done. It's too late. But they [Bomaderry Aboriginal Children's Home] never told us where we came from or who our people were, and it's too late, now, to tell us. If they had told us earlier it would have been different. But now it's been ruined.

But I love them, I really love my people. I thought I mightn't accept them but they all just came up to me, shaking hands and saying, 'Hi sis,' or 'Hi cos, how are you,' 'Hi Aunt'—and my heart went out to them. It should have happened like that years ago, and I could have been living up there with them. But now it's too hard. One old lady, she broke down and said, 'You were only a baby when they took you, I remember you two being taken away,' and a lot of them talked about it. They said, 'Oh your poor mother, they put her away,' and they are still resenting today. You wonder why, why did it happen? Might've been a purpose in it. You don't know.

Could you ever live there?

I don't know. If it was nice I would—no, I don't know. I'd like to go back and have a reunion but it's too far.

I wouldn't like to live there. I don't think that I will ever get to know my people, it's too late.

Was there a purpose?

Well as I said, I wouldn't be a missionary today [at Bomaderry] among the children. They've got a lot to learn. Their parents come and visit them here and they go home. I accept any Aborigine people. If they want a cup of tea, my door's always open to anybody. They're my people, white or brown. If I give money, I am helping them to drink, so instead I make them sandwiches and give them a cup of tea.

JOY WILLIAMS

Do you have any advice for people going home to meet their families?

I reckon they should find one of their women cousins that they're really close to and talk to them about it. You see, I talk to Helen [Janey's daughter] more about this sort of thing, because Janey is more of a mum. Helen is more of a sister and I talk to Helen about these sort of things. She's the one who has said to me, 'Look, just let these feelings flow around you, not through you, otherwise its going to destroy you.' See if I can put it a bit more simple. Yeah: find one of your women cousins, just one you are close to, and I'm sure each one of us will [find] our special one. Let things happen. Yes, and try not to stand back. Get involved in things even if you end up babysitting all the time you're there, it doesn't matter. My God, you've got the chance to look after your own babies. Let things go.

Did you make any mistakes at first?

Janey didn't have any food in the fridge, so big-hearted magnanimous wheel-barra Joy decides to put food in the fridge. So I trotted down to Coles and bought $78 worth of food, soft drinks, fruit, everything. Filled the fridge up. Half an hour later, the fuckin' thing's empty again, and now all the little kids running around with the iceblocks and stuff that I'd bought for Jane. I asked her what had happened to the food, and I said I had bought all that food for you, and she said, 'Listen girl, we share.' I understand it now. You know, since going back, I think a lot of kids up there are better fed than a lot of gub [white] kids, because when one's got, everybody's got. I've not seen those kids go hungry and they're certainly not wanting for clothes or anything, and they're not hand-me-downs from St Vinnys or Smith family. If it's too small, it's just given to another child who's in the family, that's the way it should be. I still feel awful though, 'cause one of my cousins was down here, he said I'd got too many things. And I'm wondering if I have to give it all to the poor.

What has been the best thing about coming home to Erambie?

Just the whole feeling, the whole atmosphere. Colour of the ground. This is a bit of philosophy: gubs are brought up hating blacks, right, for no particular reason. But Koories are brought up hating whites because they think, 'This is my waterhole and you've stolen it', or 'This is where my mother walked and you've stolen that.' So we can hate for specific reasons, but the gubs can't, they just hate. Sometimes I feel like that in Cowra because I think, 'My mother walked here.' Now we've got all the hateful things that have happened and now we're all coming back and we're rebuilding it. Each of our personalities and each of our pasts.

See that's another thing I had to get used to, and I'm still getting used to: the child only has had sixteen months past with my family. It's a bit like a vacuum and slowly that vacuum's being filled. Well I'm forty-two. When I first met you, you explained to me that we all have the child in us. You explained that when you go home you feel young again. I thought, 'Coral's just doing the amateur psychology here.' But it's true, because you just feel so out of control, you're not in control of the situation. At the moment you feel very very young. A lot of things come back. Things have happened in the past and you've got all these things whizzing round, and I can understand how a person could go quite insane if they weren't able to handle it. It's quite schizophrenic at times. On the one hand I follow Janey round like a puppy, like a young child. And yet I'm a woman. Any decisions that are made up there, I can be an adult and a woman. And yet I do funny little things that I don't understand even yet. I hang out to go home [to Erambie]. It's a childish thing—not childish, immature—but child-like that gets me in the car and gets me going. My expectations are very childlike. I'm in so much of a hurry to get to know everybody, really know them, and be part.

I remember you also said at Cowra they don't need me like I need them. That's changing to a degree, very subtle. Like, I can be away for two weeks, and Richard says, 'Took long enough to get you back, didn't you?'. Instead of saying, 'G'day, how are you, did you have a good drive?', he says, 'Well it took you long enough to get back.' Yes.

It's good and I'm starting to get the child-past back in me. Like, we went blackberry picking, and that's something kids would do. Well that's given me a bit of a past because I know that I've been fishing with Richard and the boys, and that's good. And air-raided by Jane: I've had me little temper tantrums up there too, don't you worry. One of Helen's boys says, 'Oh well, you're not a Murray, a Glass or a Coe.'

'What's that got to do with the price of fish?'

'Well you know the mission was given to us.'

'Tough. Now you've got to share it with another Williams.'

Are you going back to Erambie as an equal now?

Yes, and I think I'm contributing as much as I get. You

know, it's not all one-sided. Some of the things I'm told by different ones there would make your hair go all frizzy, but I don't go back and say it to a person that it's said about. No, I'm used as a sort of confidante, and a friend. Plus money-bags sometimes. I've often sat in on the card nights, and my job has always been to get the savouries ready and the pots of tea. They just sit and talk and they hear all about what the kids have been doing at school, and who's having babies, who's lost a baby, who's in gaol, who's just got out of gaol, who's down in the cop-shop, and who got bashed up the night before, where so-and-so and so-and-so has just gone down to the coast for a while and this sort of thing. It's like a little newspaper. It seems to be where the Koori post works, the Koori telegraph works, at a card game. I just listen to all the women talking around the cards and that, it's really good. No men around. They wouldn't be game, and it just seems like the women's meeting ground. The first card game I saw, I thought, 'Gawd, where'd they get the money?'. Well look, I think to meself, I'm just happy to be there. And I'm happy to be making the tea and whatever because they know I'm there. They know who I am. Sometimes I think [about] the trouble they must have to accept me in the way I am. They're trying and I'm trying.

Are there other ways that you are different now after going home?

I've never liked women very much. But that's changing slowly and I prefer to be with the women. That's where your place is. I'm getting along with women in general too, since I've been home. In fact I'm a different person up there, a lot nicer and a lot softer. You said, 'Why don't you try it down here [in Nowra]?'. I have been and it's easier. I've been making an effort to be who I really am. Funny that change when I go up there. It's just natural. And I also notice that you don't get called 'Auntie' easily. Some of the young boys didn't call me anything at all, and then I went up again, and all of a sudden they were all calling me 'Auntie Joy'. I love it. Love it. And I think

I've earned it too. Not just given.

I have had to learn, and I'm still learning, that you don't live by a clock. You know, I used to think 'Koori' time was just an excuse for laziness, but it's not. Koori time to me, is you just eat when you're hungry, you sleep where you are, you wake up when you've had enough sleep and go to bed when you're tired. Not at nine o'clock or whatever. That's how you live down here.

Did you ever imagine that you'd be sitting down with the other women talking about babies?

No! No way. It was worse than Avon or Tupperware. It was horrible. In fact, I used studiously to avoid pregnant women, or women with young children because that's all you'd hear. [But now] Well, they're mine. They're mine too. I'm just as much part of those babies as she is. It's just not in me to say, 'How are they?', or 'Has Nat had his immunisation?', or something like that. I just do it, just comes out.

Can you put in a nutshell what going home was all about?

Sometimes when I'm home by myself I cry, and it's just being home, and I know I'm going again. Just thinking about Janey and how big she is, not just inside, but how big she is in my life. I still get angry though. For being deprived of them. But then I mightn't have been ready a few years ago. See I can't imagine being without Cowra now. I don't want to be without Cowra. I've no intention of being without Cowra. It affects every part of my personality. It affects what I want to do tomorrow. It affects me today. I know where I'm going to die, which helps. That's not being morbid, but I know I'm going back there and I know what will happen there, and it's good.

Paul Behrendt

In tracing my own links and in doing so, having to go through the cobwebs of missing parts, I realised how fragmented Aboriginal society had become, and why it was so hard for people who had the desire to trace their roots on their own—without any outside help. As I progressed I heard more and more stories of how people were taken away and how families were broken up, I think that with my experience I can understand the feelings of people who are in this turmoil and I can offer help—support—and encouragement to them. I have been a fairly resilient person and I have stood by myself all through life, but with Link-Up I have found people with whom I have an understanding—people with whom I shared something. They have been through something that, unless you have experienced it, is very hard to understand.

There's always been something there. What I feel most of all is the desire to grab hold of the last thread. With people like Ivy Green, or other people in their late sixties—I can touch them and say, 'I have touched Ivy Green and Ivy Green has touched the past.' Of course, Ivy Green herself also touched my mother, and that is very precious to me.

Is there some kind of force driving you now?

Yes. The word I'm looking for is somewhere between obligation and compulsion. A duty, perhaps? But then again I guess that is an obligation. It's very hard to define, but I have that inner drive to hammer the story of the outrageous things that have happened to the Aboriginal people until it has been accepted as an established part of the official history of this country.

Today when you say to the ordinary person in the street, 'Look what happened,' they either say they didn't know or that it didn't happen because it isn't written down in the history books. The only way to get the full story is

Paul with Ivy Green. Ivy Green was Paul's mother's cousin. This photograph was taken while she was showing Paul around his ancestral country.

to talk to the people who were involved. You can't rely on Protection Board documents. How can you possibly get the story of children taken away from their home without talking to the people themselves? The important thing is to record their story now, and even if it is not used for ten, twenty or even 100 years, the story will still be there. But if we don't record it now, then it will never come out at all.

Is there something which binds together all the people who have been removed from their families?

Yes. Even today in depressed Aboriginal communities such as Walgett or Brewarrina, the youths cannot understand people being taken away the way that they were. They cannot understand why they let people take their children away. But the reason why they cannot understand is that they were not brought up in, nor could they ever comprehend living in, the environment that existed in the days when such activities were actually written into law. So there in itself exists a bond between people who can say, 'Here is somebody who has been through what I have been through and has suffered what I have suffered, and who understands the scars that it has left on me.' And while people who have not been touched by it often say quite genuinely that they understand this hurt, it is somewhat akin to a man saying that he understands the pain of childbirth, when it is something that only a woman can completely know. I guess that is the bond which people in Link-Up have.

RICK MCLEOD

Rick McLeod, Pauline McLeod, Michael, Rachel, their mother June and many other relatives had spent their first weekend together in Sydney. When Rick returned to Brisbane, June accompanied him for a holiday.

Did you find out anything about your Dad?

Yeah, Robert told me a bit, and talking to Mum. Had a bit of a chat, 'What did Dad look like?' and all this stuff, and she sent some photos up. When his name was mentioned she just sort of shut up, so it was, 'Don't mention the name when you're round her.' If she wanted to talk about it she would bring it up herself. And she did. When she came up for a week she let loose a little bit, had a bit of a chat and a bit of a laugh. You didn't force things. Well, that's the way Mum was.

Did you find out what happened to your brother Ronnie?

Robert told me. Apparently he was with foster parents, and he was riding home on his pushbike and he got hit by a car, and he was in a coma for a couple of days and eventually died.

So how were you feeling after your Mum came to stay?

I felt I could live with myself a lot more. A lot more comfortable with myself. It was just nice to be accepted for what you are. Happy, for one, because you've really come to terms with your own identity. And enjoying the fact that Aboriginals have got so many family and relations who have always been there. You can call me a black bastard or anything and it doesn't affect me whatsoever now. It's only taken twenty-three years! There's no stigma any more. Plus my own kids. I tell them they're Aboriginal. I tell my kids the things I missed out on, so at least they're getting told. The more I talk about it, the better I feel, so there's an identity there.

JEANETTE SINCLAIR

Jeanette Sinclair had returned to Perth, with her daughter Sharmane, to meet her mother and family for the first time.

I got [back to Sydney] and then I thought about it and then I thought it hadn't been all I wanted it to be. And I felt Mum and I were friends but I got the feeling—it wasn't even a feeling—I just knew we were never going to be like I wanted us to be, mother and daughter, and I was never going to have the feeling of laying on her, on her chest sort of feeling I was talking about earlier. I suppose it really hurt me a lot because I wanted that. And I was really drained for a month after I came back and then I started going back to Tranby, getting stuck into the work I was supposed to be doing, and then without realising it I started blocking thinking about Mum altogether. I didn't think about her, I didn't write, I didn't telephone. And I didn't realise it at the time, but after four or five months being back, I started getting on the self-destruct cycle again. I had no energy, nothing. I wasn't thinking, I was a big blank nothing.

I was sitting home here one weekend thinking about

where I was going now and what help it had been going home to see Mum and then I realised the reason I hadn't rung her up was I was testing her to see whether she really loved me. If she rang me up, she must care, if she didn't ring me then she didn't. Which was rather stupid, childish. But nobody said you're an adult after you go to see your mother, or when you get back, either. I mean, I behaved very childishly and I thought about it, and I thought, 'That's really fucking stupid.' And I rang her up and said, 'Hi, it's me.' And she hadn't rang because she thought that, one, she was invading my privacy, and two, that maybe I, after seeing her, didn't like what I had seen and so therefore didn't want to see her anymore.

Was it hard to go back a second time?

Yes it was. I was a nervous wreck going back the second time. At least I had a plane to get me there this time and Mum met me at the airport. We went back to the house, and things weren't as good the second time round as they were the first time around. There were gaps in conversation again. It seemed like we'd talked out all the areas that could be talked about without encroaching on each other's space. So it was a bit difficult the first few days I was over there until we both relaxed a bit and things came back and it was like I'd lived there all the time. It was funny and it was OK.

Was it easier to identify as Aboriginal in Sydney now?

Yes. It was, because I had somebody I could say, 'That's mine, that's my crowd over there, that's my mob, I belong here.' And I knew some names, and when people talked about them I could put a picture to that name, a character to that name. I thought, 'This is wonderful.' It was great. I had somewhere I belonged. That was really great and it was like that hole you walked around with had been totally filled. The first time I went back, that's what it was like although I realise now it can never be really filled in. Ninety per cent of the hole can be filled in but I think you are always missing that ten per cent. That's just my personal opinion. You can never get the ten per cent back because you have missed out on the bonding, the fondling and the cuddling. Also you've missed out on building relationships over a period of time: you can't create a relationship out of thin air. And all the trust and everything when it comes dealing with family, like cousins, takes time. It takes time on a continual basis and unless you move in next door you can't get those relationships going.

Were there Koories who refused to understand?

There were a few, they said we were blacks that we were jumping on the bandwagon. Two of the worst offenders were the darkest girl in the college and the lightest girl in the college. One of them wanted to punch my face in for the first two months I was there. Then Link-Up came and gave a talk and it turned out alright because after she had been shown what had actually happened, and I put my hand up and said, 'Yes I've been through that,' her whole attitude changed.

Also, those white friends I had before I no longer have. It was horrible, still is sometimes, left in limbo when you don't have those white friendships because you had to get rid of them because they were a burden to you, and then you haven't made any black friends, and so you're friendless. You have nobody and that's where Tranby became important, in supplying those friends. And there were people there that became so tolerant because, even though they had lived in the Aboriginal community all their life, they accepted things happening in their lives [even though] they didn't understand the reasons behind them. They knew people got taken but they didn't know why because a lot of older people wouldn't talk about it. Tranby gave them the reasons why. They became very tolerant towards me and very understanding and compassionate. They wouldn't say things in front of me that I wouldn't understand. So I wasn't left in the situation where I felt everybody was talking a different language. That made a lot of difference.

What have you been doing since you left Tranby?

I'm out at NSW University because I came to realise that I wasn't as dumb as everyone told me I was. Through Tranby I got into the university and decided to do some sort of a course that would give me the ability to be able to do counselling because I wanted to work with people that have been in the same situation as myself. I get my degree next year. What a thought! Not bad for somebody that only went to sixth grade at primary school. I never get over it, but I mean, there's a whole bunch of us up there that are like that.

Nancy De Vries

A lot of them try to understand, a lot of them are well aware of their history. But it's the younger generation that's growing up, that didn't know what happened in those days, to them it's just like history. To some young people it's very remote, it's not part of their life. So they find it very difficult to understand, because they had the privilege of growing up with their families. These young people cannot understand the agony, the loneliness, the need, the want, the mental torment—and they don't want to know, a lot of them. They are all too wrapped up in what's happening today, but they forget that the struggle is still going on for these people who are lost. To get home. To get home, to belong, to be able to identify.

How many Koories who have been lost, who have found their way home, are now working in the field of Aboriginal education, welfare, health, and who are holding top positions in these areas? They've got skills, they've got love, they've got the joy of being home, they want to be able to say, 'Right, whatever those gubbas [whites] have taught us, let's put it to some use, back to our people.' I've learned skills in my life but I have never ever lost sight of the fact that I'm an Aborigine first and foremost. That is why I am now working in the Aboriginal Medical Service. I've finished my training, I'm very proud of that. I've achieved something. I wanted my poor old mother to be so proud of me, that here was one who'd been lost but she'd managed to achieve something. I wanted her to know and to understand why I'm working with my people: it's just the sheer joy of being in my country. It's my area, it's my home, it's my land, it's me. Suddenly I know that it's me, that land. It's just something special.

I think that we [Link-Up people] have got a very important role to play in Aboriginal society, and I hope that people in the communities that have a person who's been lost and come home, can greet them with love. We always feel that although we're lost there's a place for us waiting, and I like to think that communities can say, 'Yes, your place is here, we've been waiting for you to come home.' That's what most of us hope for, most of us wish for. But it is a culture shock for kids who have been brought up in white man's way, white man's values, taught in schools and in society their attitudes towards Aboriginal people—no good, drunks, this and that—you've only learned negative things. And suddenly you find out that you can go home to your community, it's a culture shock. I was lucky enough to have identified all my life and was able to go from strength to strength that way, that was one of the things that kept me going. But these kids who've had their whole lives stuffed up by these families—it's very very hard.

[People in communities] have got to remember that they have had their kids taken away from them, it's true, but what did the kids have taken from them? They've got to realise that we lost our way of talking that is distinctly Aboriginal, it's a wonderful wonderful thing to listen to. I envy them that they can speak like this, but I can never copy it. I still feel apart because I can't talk like this. We had love taken away from us. The families still had some form of support, but the child that was taken away had none. Even if brothers and sisters were taken away, they were split up.

I don't give a stuff what anybody says, one of the biggest tragedies in this life is for someone to grow up totally without love. As a child, growing up without anybody ever opening their arms to them and saying, 'Don't cry.' I never had that luxury, and the majority of us never had that luxury. [Instead] they make you feel in debt to them for giving you a good white home. Load of bullshit. I loved my mother, I loved my mother, I have loved my mother since I can remember. It was just the thought of finding my mother that kept me going. I didn't know my mother but I loved my mother. They probably think, 'Oh that silly old bugger, what's she raving on about?', but they wouldn't know because they've never been without their mother.

To people that haven't found their families yet, I'd say: look at yourself first. Say, 'I am an Aborigine.' Think about it. 'I belong somewhere, and I think it's about time I found out just where I fit into this society.' Doesn't matter how long it takes, how many times you see sisters and brothers meeting each other and you cry inside—but you're happy for them—and you're jealous—don't stop. When you think that you're at a dead end, that you'll never get over it, don't give up. Even when you find them and you begin to have doubts, don't give up.

Even if your poor old mother won't accept you or she's got a lot of problems she's had to live through, the drama and trauma of losing a child. When you get to my age it's pretty hard to relate a crooked old body here with her baby. But don't give up.

THE CONTRIBUTORS

(Notes supplied by contributors)

ALICIA ADAMS was an assistant at the United Aborigines Mission Home at Bomaderry, New South Wales until 1988.

SHERRY ATKINSON is a student of Performing Arts at Eora College, Sydney. She does modelling, acting and community radio work. She is living in Sydney, hopes to become an actress and sees her family frequently.

PAUL BEHRENDT is an Aboriginal Fellow in the Faculty of Liberal Studies at the University of New South Wales.

STAN BOWDEN is a co-worker at Link-Up. He feels more settled now than he ever has in his whole life. He knows who he is and what he is. He feels a lot better because he's helping other people through the same problems that he faced all his life.

SHARON CARPENTER worked voluntarily as an announcer for Aboriginal radio station Radio Redfern in 1986 and 1987. She currently works part-time as a singer and actress. Her hopes for the future are to expand her career as a singer and through the arts contribute to the struggle of Aboriginal people.

JEAN CARTER is the founder and Co-ordinator of Jilimi Women's Centre, Nowra.

KIM CHAPMAN, since her first visit, has met her brother Carl and his family. They are very compatible and get on very well. She is working in Sydney as a trainee in community work, and hopes to go to university and become a social worker.

PAUL CREMEN works for the Shoalhaven Shire Council.

NANCY DE VRIES is the graduate registered nurse at the Aboriginal Health Service, Brewarrina. She feels that she has finally come home.

CORAL EDWARDS is the founder and current Co-ordinator of Link-Up.

PAULINE MCLEOD is now in her second year at college, doing a Bachelor of Arts in Social Sciences. She hopes to be a qualified lecturer in Aboriginal Studies one day. She writes: 'A lot has happened in the last year. Mum and Robert died a year after we met and my foster parents disowned me completely. I have come a long way to find my Aboriginality and as an Aboriginal person I have survived. I couldn't wait any longer because if I had missed Mum or Robert as well it would have killed me. As such I met them, I love them and I am so glad I went home.'

RICK MCLEOD, since he has found his identity, has become more community-oriented. He is currently working for the Link-Up program in Queensland.

PETER READ is a former co-worker at Link-Up. He is currently a Research Fellow in History in the Research School of Social Sciences at the Australian National University in Canberra.

JEANETTE SINCLAIR is a part-time youth worker with some of New South Wales' most sexually, emotionally and physically abused children. It is very draining work! She is also a full-time student at the University of New South Wales. She hopes to have her Bachelor of Arts in Sociology at the end of 1989.

JOY WILLIAMS was eighteen when she left the Home and feels she has lost her years there. Currently she is a third year Bachelor of Arts, English/History student at Wollongong University and is the Regional Representative of the Aboriginal Educational Consultative Group. She is involved with the Aboriginal Community Centre in Wollongong and with the Royal Commission into Black Deaths in Custody. Her main goal is to get Black Literature placed at all levels of education.